Mac Miller B

A Tribute to a Musical Genius

James Raymon Gunn

TABLE OF CONTENTS

INTRODUCTION

2018-05-17, Mac Miller was present in a bar. He was having a couple drinks while out with buddies. He was in a good place back then. He was content since he was dating Ariana Grande, one of the most well-known singers in the world. His fourth album, The Divine Feminine, which was released in the fall of 2016, had gotten good reviews, and he had recently given a career-highlight performance at Coachella.

But most importantly, that period of his life was over after years of drug misuse. The way of life had been very successful for him. He had already amassed a large following at that point thanks to the release of four studio albums, a ton of mixtapes, and several collaborations.

He had begun on his own with Rostrum Records before switching to a larger company, Warner Bros., and signing a 10 million dollar deal. Success, however, had not been simple. He was a white rapper from Pittsburgh, Pennsylvania who performed in a primarily Black musical genre; respect wasn't given; it had to be won, and it required effort. He spent years pounding the pavement, touring incessantly, and releasing music in an effort to be taken seriously.

However, the couple maintained appearances and it appeared that most of their followers were in favor of their relationship. They appeared at events together, performed at each other's concerts, and were sighted on each other's social media pages. Things looked to be going well for a year and a half, but then, well, they weren't.

By the time the seventeenth came around—the day Mac sat at that bar—a week had passed. During that time, reports about Ariana and Pete's new relationship swept the gossip pages, and the engaged couple did little to quell them. Instead, they merely stirred the water while flirting in the manner that best represented their generation: by liking one other's older Instagram photographs and sharing pictures of their matching tattoos.

He lived not far from the bar. It was so close, in fact, that he saw no issue with leaving that bar with his car keys in hand, putting those keys into the ignition of his white 2014 Mercedes G63 AMG—the "G-Wagon," as it is colloquially known—and doing something they tell you not to do when you've been drinking, let alone drinking the way Mac was known to drink. He would later tell his longtime DJ, Clockwork, that it was "mad close."

Mac Miller swung open the G-Wagon's driver-side door and stepped outside into the night. He fled through a fence, managed to get away, and was subsequently apprehended at his home on suspicion of DUI and hit-and-run. The following day, he was released after posting a $15,000 bail.

However, the crash seemed unexpected. Maybe it was a message.

He continued to work on the record that would become Swimming just over a week after the crash as he sat in the backyard of his Brentwood home, gazing out at the mountains, the vast sky above, and the row of houses constructed below. He found immense peace in the view most mornings.

Chapter 1

The Pittsburgh neighborhood of Point Breeze has tidy, green streets and calm, tranquil air. Pristine, well-kept blocks are dotted with grand mansions. You may assume that keeping one's lawn is the most obvious challenge present.

Back then, the Greensburg Pike, a Native American trail that had been paved in the early nineteenth century, was the only route through Point Breeze. The Pittsburgh gentry soon discovered the area, which was at once rural and distant; they saw it as a sanctuary from the noise and bustle of the city that was fast expanding around it. This was not long after the area was paved.

Judge William Wilkins was one of the distinguished people that arrived in Point Breeze. Wilkins, whose father served as a captain in the American Revolution, held a number of high-profile roles. In his day, he was somewhat of a big deal. He served as the president of the Bank of Pittsburgh, a member of the House of Representatives, a senator, a congressman, the secretary of defense, and even the US ambassador to Russia.

Wilkins entertained distinguished visitors at Homewood. Daniel Webster, Henry Clay, and even John Calhoun, the seventh vice president of the United States, stopped by the home for lunch and conversation because, you know, politics. While this was going on, Point Breeze and Homewood's surrounding environment were undergoing tremendous change. Pittsburgh was a young city and America as a whole was a young nation. But it was already showing to be one of the Union's most crucial locations.

The Ohio River, which originated at the meeting of the Allegheny and Monongahela Rivers and traveled 981 miles southwest to Cairo,

Illinois, where it joined the Mississippi, is located near Pittsburgh. Because railroads were still in their infancy and people were still getting around by going on the waterways in the early 1800s, Pittsburgh's main industry was boats.

Andrew Carnegie was arguably the most well-known of the Pittsburgh aspirants. Carnegie was born in Scotland, but after his parents experienced financial difficulty early in his infancy, they borrowed money and relocated to Pennsylvania in 1848 with Andrew. They moved into "slab town," a noisy, packed immigrant neighborhood with only the greatest amenities. There was no water or natural gas, and the streets were always completely dark at night. There were also wild hogs and wandering dogs everywhere.

Having enough money to no longer be impoverished but still lacking in certain ways the amenities that wealth could provide, Carnegie composed a message to himself in his early thirties. It was never disclosed during his lifetime; it was only made public after his passing when his wife gave it to the New York Public Library. The memo outlined Carnegie's plans to retire at age 35. At that time, he would strive to become a learned, sophisticated man. By the time he was forty, his mind would be flush with all the literary knowledge he had since then consumed. Carnegie imagined moving to London in his newly cosmopolitan life to focus on more serious issues; perhaps he would run a newspaper while using his money wisely to help those who were less fortunate.

Early retirement, however, was never taken. A few years later, Carnegie started making steel out of iron, which prompted him to acquire steel factories. He founded Carnegie Steel Company in the late 1800s, and in 1901, at J. P. Morgan's request, he sold it to U.S. Steel for 226 million dollars, which is now equivalent to more than $7 billion.

In fact, Henry Clay Frick invited Theodore Roosevelt in 1902 as part of an executive group trying to bring the president to Pittsburgh. Roosevelt agreed and soon after arrived in the city, where he addressed an audience of more than 750,000 people at Schenley Park. He then left for Clayton instead of going back to Washington so he could have dinner with the Fricks. Both the Fricks' house and Point Breeze were enticing in this way. Its streets have seen presidents.

Early retirement, however, was never taken. A few years later, Carnegie started making steel out of iron, which prompted him to acquire steel factories. He founded Carnegie Steel Company in the late 1800s, and in 1901, at J. P. Morgan's request, he sold it to U.S. Steel for 226 million dollars, which is now equivalent to more than $7 billion.

In fact, Henry Clay Frick invited Theodore Roosevelt in 1902 as part of an executive group trying to bring the president to Pittsburgh. Roosevelt agreed and soon after arrived in the city, where he addressed an audience of more than 750,000 people at Schenley Park. He then left for Clayton instead of going back to Washington so he could have dinner with the Fricks. Both the Fricks' house and Point Breeze were enticing in this way. Its streets have seen presidents.

Chapter 2

On January 19, 1992, at 8:46 A.M., Malcolm McCormick was born. He weighed precisely eight pounds. And it appeared he was doomed to draw notice ever after that day.

Mark, however, was not a native of Pittsburgh; rather, he had spent his formative years in the affluent Akron suburb of Silver Lake, Ohio. He earned a psychology and philosophy degree from Miami University of Ohio in the early 1970s. He returned to school after some time spent working as a carpenter in Denver, Colorado, and earned a master's in architecture in 1979.

Mark got work with Barker Rinker Seacat & Partners in Denver quite quickly. In 1984, he was made a partner, but it wasn't long before he was moving again, this time to Pennsylvania. By that time, he had already met Pittsburgh-born Karen, and the two of them got hitched in 1986.4 Karen attended Boston University and Emerson College specifically where she studied English and art history. Her mother was a housewife and her father was an engineer.

The family's first child was given the name Miller, possibly in honor of his maternal grandmother Marcia, who was born Marcia Miller before taking the last name of both her first and second husbands, Mickey Weiss and William "Ted" Meyers (which Karen appears to have adopted and kept when she married Mark).

The McCormick family had a successful early 1990s. By that time, Mark had quit his work in the city and returned to the private sector, purchasing Oliver Design Group, his former employer. The Heinz 57 Center, a historic structure that originally housed Gimbels' premier department store and was renamed under the corporate name of German ketchup inventor and former Point Breeze resident Henry J. Heinz, was one of Mark's major undertakings when Malcolm arrived in 1992.

Most of the time, Malcolm had a perfect upbringing. The family relocated to a new, larger house with five bedrooms in 1998, a few blocks away. Everything was going fine. A few years prior, Mark had finished a sizable project: the renovation of the city library in the Pittsburgh suburb of Mount Lebanon.

The post-hippie generation, which dominated most of American life in the second half of the 20th century, included Karen and Mark as baby boomers. They were interested in all forms of art, music, and culture. When the children were small, they brought them to jazz performances in the park; at home, they introduced the boys to music from their own youth and other genres that appealed to them.

Malcolm loved music in general, and his favorite record over time was Sgt. Pepper's Lonely Hearts Club Band by the Beatles. Malcolm had two Beatles tattoos—John Lennon on his right forearm and the phrase "Imagine" on his right inner bicep—as a result of his intense affection for the band.

As soon as Malcolm was old enough to understand music, he became fascinated in it. He would move to any beat in the house and would frequently be seen dancing. Then, when they were five or six years old, things really ramped up. He wasn't particularly looking forward to another pair of socks during the holiday season.

Then there was religion, the cornerstone of every child's upbringing. Dad was Catholic, and Mom was Jewish. This made things difficult for Malcolm, like it did for many children of interfaith marriages. His idea of who he was was ephemeral and formed by the environment.

He attended Catholic schools in his early years. At St. Peter & Paul, it began with elementary school. The next step is middle school at St. Bede, where the emphasis is placed on "Faith, Family, Community, Love, and Service" and where the guiding principle is "that each child is a unique human being endowed by God with special gifts."

In the end, the objective was to serve as an example of "Christ-like behaviors through actions and words." Malcolm, though, also attended Hebrew school. At the age of thirteen, he celebrated his bar mitzvah at the revered Rodef Shalom21, the oldest Jewish congregation in western Pennsylvania.

Another former camp director, Jeremy Goldman, recalled telling Malcolm that his favorite song was "Send Me on My Way" by Rusted Root in an interview with the Chronicle. And sure enough, Malcolm was there with the guitar, singing the song on Saturday night. He was cooler than anyone I had ever met when he was 13 years old, and I was 31 at the time, according to Goldman. "He always brought the house down when it was his turn to perform his act."

He has the Jewish symbol for a Chai tattooed on the upper left arm. Chet and Yod, the two letters that make up the Chai in Judaism, are supposed to together mean "alive" or "living." The Chai honors existence.

He had two motives for getting the tattoo. He wanted it to serve as a reminder of what a Jew he was. But it's also important to keep in mind that no moment in life is more important than another; simply being alive and breathing is a wonderful thing.

He hoped he would never take life for granted.

Chapter 3

In Point Breeze, things were perfect. It was a "front porch" neighborhood where neighbors watched over one another's children. When an adult suspected someone from the "other side"—say, from neighboring Homewood, which is just across Penn Avenue—of scoping out the neighborhood, they would walk over and let them know they were being watched, assuming they hadn't already gotten the hint.

The area of town that was arguably the most liberal was home to many academics and artists. However, despite its relative safety and liberal politics, this area had its own challenges, including some

11

parents' tendency to keep their children on a tight leash. Malcolm was one of several youngsters in the area who avoided trouble but pushed the envelope.

Malcolm was a daring young man who was already immersed in hip-hop, which is renowned for its adult themes. Outkast's Aquemini was the first rap album he ever listened to; he found it while perusing his brother's CD collection. The record acted as a sort of compass for him.

He cherished Aquemini's fundamental topic, which was one of its best qualities. Although the subject matter was varied, the music had a distinct tone and a genuine sound; the tracks are jam-packed with live instruments and have an experimental, hallucinogenic feel. The album, which was released in 1998, went against the grain at a time when Southern rap was still in its infancy. Wu-Tang, Bad Boy, Ruff Ryderz, or Roc-A-Fella weren't involved. Outkast was playing. A work of art, too.

James Rudolph, a fellow student at St. Bede, remembered, "One of my final middle school recollections is of him with long, curly hair with a guitar under his arm while performing some Dave Matthews song to a lady at our school. There was no diamond-studded pendant or hip-hop bling hanging around his neck. Even more, "I even think he was wearing a puka-shell necklace, those bead necklaces that were a hallmark of the early 2000s, while he was doing it."

He performed with bands and even took part in certain regional tournaments. He sang and played the acoustic guitar at a battle of the bands in 2004 that was held at the Jewish Community Center; those who were present recall it being an outstanding little performance. Perhaps there was hope for this. He may develop a successful rock career as an adult, touring college campuses while playing guitar in a jam band.

But the dream of the band was postponed. People didn't like his voice; it was an acquired taste. Eventually, he began to express himself in other ways.

Chapter 4

Malcolm had a wide variety of friends when he was younger. On the one hand, his friends from Point Breeze and the neighboring areas; on the other, the wonderful Jewish youngsters he attended camp with in West Virginia.
Derek Green was one of his closest pals. Marina, Derek's mother, was raised in Pittsburgh. Her father, Wesley Posvar, was Derek's grandfather; his grandmother, Mildred Miller, was a mezzo-soprano with the Metropolitan Opera who later established the Opera Theater of Pittsburgh. Wesley Posvar was a decorated air force veteran who later served as the chancellor of the University of Pittsburgh.

Karen, the mother of Malcolm, attended middle school with Derek's mother. Her marriage caused the family to start relocating frequently. Every few years, as part of his employment as a sports television producer, his father would move the entire family to a new location. After living in different states for a while—New York for a year, Maryland the following, then Oklahoma—the parents ultimately divorced. And that's when they returned to Pittsburgh.

Even then, there was something unique about Malcolm that stood out. He had a really "old soul," Brian remarked. "Despite his long time on Earth, he felt more in touch with the fundamentals of human interaction and emotion when he was a child. Even those who were much older than him could relate to him. He would be cool with seniors in high school while I was in high school—ninth or tenth grade—dappin' 'em up and cutting' with them. He performed above his years.

Things were a little more strained the next time their paths met. They were visiting Brian's grandparents' country house in Ligonier, Pennsylvania, an hour southeast of Pittsburgh, on a weekend. It's Malcolm and Derek and a number of their middle school buddies, together with Brian and Bill and a number of their high school friends. For some reason, Bill made the decision to consume acid. Bill added, "And we were just trippin' our balls out." Without being on acid, Malcolm and his friends were up to their own particular brand of mischief in a different part of the home.

Malcolm had never harbored any resentment. He didn't dress that way. He was too laid-back, lighthearted, and optimistic about people. He had no capacity for malice.

After that came TreeJ. Despite living within a fifteen-minute drive from Malcolm's home in Pittsburgh's Hill District, TreeJ spent most of her childhood there. TreeJ stated, "Up there, they sell drugs their entire lives and end up in jail." In the Hill District, everyone only does that. I had some luck getting away.3
That result was brought about by a fortunate and unlucky combination for TreeJ.

Following that, TreeJ's mother informed him that she would transfer him to a much better school. He would have to ride a bus there, but perhaps it would place him in the appropriate setting for learning and in the company of the right people to put him on a better course. She warned him, "I'm just going to whoop your ass," if he messed up once more.

The pals stayed at Derek's house a lot. There wasn't much parental control in the house, so it was a rather carefree environment. There, they would consume marijuana, enjoy music (Lil Wayne and Dipset had a lot of airplay), and generally act up.

He dropped out of school since it didn't interest him much. It wasn't anything like, "Oh, I'm rich, I don't need to do this," he remarked. "I just finished doing that and thought, 'Eh, fuck school.'" At that time, I wasn't considering my future; instead, I was merely acting rashly.

Brian left his home and moved in with Bill, where he stayed for a few months. In order to save money for an apartment, he took a job washing dishes at Point Brugge restaurant for $8 per hour. He would write rhymes in the morning before work and at night when he got home as he planned the beginning of a rap career.

The most significant room, though, was a small room with two extra beds placed side by side with stars hanging from the ceiling. When the lights were off, the stars shone brightly, and the boys would sit there looking up at them while stoned on acid, cannabis, mushrooms, or anything else they could get their hands on that day.

He watched stoner comedies like How High, featuring Redman and Method Man, and played video games. He saw the movie so frequently that he knew every line. He indulged in forty-ounce beers while making out with neighborhood women. The Star Room was where he landed his first blow job. And after losing his virginity to a girl in the basement of her parents' house while watching Nacho Libre at the age of fourteen, to whom his elder brother, Miller, as well as a few of his friends, had already had sex7, it was inside the Star Room that he had sex for the second time.

It was simple to understand why this location was a teen's dream. The boys would be hanging out in the attic on a usual night, Malcolm recalled. They had no money and were young. But they would want to use drugs. Girls in the area were aware of the Star Room. They would then dial the house.

Once a girl stopped by. She started stripping off all of her clothes since she was so high on acid. When she was finished, she sat on the couch in her undies. Malcolm said there were twenty guys in the room, and she was game for anything.

They pushed the girl into a closet after Derek's mother entered the room. No, ma'am, there is nothing wrong going on here. They began to laugh when Derek's mother left. They had to remove her from such a situation. She then left the house and got into a car to be driven to a friend's residence. Avoiding a crisis.

He shared two versions of the same story during his appearance on MTV's When I Was 17, one clean and one unpublishable by today's standards. He pleaded with the interviewer to use the dirty version, though. From this early interview, it was obvious that he was already aware that two versions of the same event might exist and that, given the choice, most people would pick the version with less edge.

The Star Room was primarily well-known for one thing, though. Malcolm McCormick really developed as a rapper there. He was unable to stop.

Chapter 5

In the attic of Derek Green's home one day when he was fourteen years old, Malcolm was freestyling as he often did in his spare time. On this particular day, Derek took out a Canon PowerShot camera and started recording Malcolm while he was simply having fun. After finishing, Derek sent Brian the video via email.

Malcolm was a talented rapper, and Brian was pleased. Technically speaking, they weren't particularly strong. Simple lyrical exercise using rhymes for related words, as rappers do. The speed at which Malcolm came up with ideas for rap songs was what ultimately convinced Brian. Freestyling, specifically true freestyling, in which a rapper creates lyrics on the fly, is considered to be a lost art form since it started to lose favor in the middle of the 1990s. Malcolm, though, was standing there dropping bars off the top of his head.

Nils was a friend of Brian's at the time. Nils was one of those kids who, if you hung around with him for a while, would ultimately want to start a cypher even though he was abjectly terrible at rapping. We need to invite him over so he can freestyle, Nils added. So they extended an invitation to Malcolm to visit Brian's flat, which is located next to the Star Room.

All of the songs were essentially "freestyles" in the contemporary definition of the phrase, consisting of instrumental pieces with written words overlaid. You could create a mixtape if you collected enough of these freestyles. Sometimes a mixtape would contain original tracks and feel like an album in its entirety. It occasionally included both freestyles and original music. A mixtape might be purchased, but they could also be given away for free as marketing materials. In the end, there was no set method for making a mixtape. They served as the public's equivalent of demo recordings for a budding young artist, saying to anybody who came into possession of one: Hey, I'm a rapper, check me out!

He dressed in an enormous blue and gold Pittsburgh Panthers basketball jersey for the cover. He had a blue fitting cap with the rear twisted on his head. He entered the Star Room and took a seat on the bed. Malcolm didn't care that it was covered in papers and spindles of CD-Rs. He raised both fists while trying to be a tough guy and bit his lower lip. He then instructed Brian to take a photo.

Despite the mixtape's rarity, according to Kalson, those who heard it immediately recognized Mac's skill. The mixtape was unprofessional. But everyone who heard it thought that he was humorous, charming, and exceptionally talented for his age. He made it when he was around 14 years old.

The mixtape's original copies are hard to come by. There is a nine-track version available online, but that isn't the real mixtape. You can listen to it on YouTube or the website DatPiff. Instead, Malcolm simply uploaded a selection of tracks on DatPiff because he thought the original version was so terrible. The mixtape itself is much worse than the online version, according to Brian.

Malcolm was greatly let down if he had anticipated that But My Mackin' Ain't Easy would transform his life. At the prep school he was currently attending, Winchester Thurston, it garnered him considerable interest. But that was all there was.

A block and a half from Malcolm's house, the former proprietors of the Frick Park Market recall him bringing the mixtapes around and attempting to sell them to neighborhood youngsters after school.

The proprietors, a husband and wife, provided assistance even though they weren't really enthusiastic. The husband would make jokes with Malcolm about how bad his early music was and tell him he needed to improve.

But becoming a popular rapper wasn't something to take lightly. Malcolm would need to put in a lot more effort to improve if he wanted to stand out. Anyone with a computer may now create a mixtape in their bedroom thanks to technology. And that bedroom-style look would go on to define a lot of the music that would go on to become famous in the future.

Malcolm and Brian got along well at work. They frequently exchanged lyrics back and forth during recording. Brian would rhyme a few lines after Malcolm did, and they would continue in this manner, their two separate voices serving the same sound. This was a common practice among classic hip-hop acts like EPMD, A Tribe Called Quest, and Kid 'n Play.

The notion of forming a group quickly came to fruition. Brian recalled, "We were simply like, 'Yo, we should just fuckin' make a group. "One day, very late at night, I drove my car out to meet him at his mother's house. He mentioned something about "the Ill Spoken" as we were going to discuss some stuff. That crap is kind of like a group name, I remarked. The Ill Spoken is some backpacker-sounding stuff. That ended the matter.

Kalson truly enjoyed Malcolm's music when he first heard it. Kalson was a dedicated fan of hip-hop. He possessed an almost encyclopedic understanding of the various rap scenes in various places. He was aware of everything going on in "the culture," including new producers and performers.

He told Brian that Malcolm had impressed him, and Brian then passed that knowledge along to his young padawan. Kalson returned home from college for the winter break in late 2007. When Malcolm entered, he was with Brian.

According to the resume, Kalson lacked the necessary qualifications for management. Certainly not in the conventional sense. He had no experience working for a record company and had few contacts in the business. He was however technologically savvy and eager. He paid close attention to what was going on at RapMullet.com's forums since during that time, in the mid-2000s, many well-known mixtape DJs would peruse the forums looking for fresh music.

Tuff Sound is the name of the location where they recorded. It was managed out of the home of an engineer named Soy Sos, who lived on Trenton Avenue in Wilkinsburg, a neighborhood close to Pittsburgh. It was technically still within the Pittsburgh metro area and only a short distance from Point Breeze, but living in a community with a median family income of $26,621 made it feel like a whole other place from the streets Malcolm had known growing up.

Soy was dubious. He was grown and born in Pittsburgh, thus he was familiar with the town and had collaborated with several of its hip-hop musicians. The majority (though by no means all) were from the Hill District, Braddock, Garfield, and Homewood. The fantasy of being a famous rapper persisted in these Black neighborhoods because, like professional athletics, it might offer a path out of the ghetto.

Then there was the Ill Spoken, Easy Mac, and B-Dub (later Beedie), the name Brian had given himself, who was white and hailed from the seedy neighborhoods of Point Breeze.

If not their lack of talent, he would have been upset by another thing that white rappers would do. Like one Braddock gang that was predominantly Black but contained a single White person. Soy stated, "His name was Tony, but they nicknamed him White Tone and gave him permission to use the N-word. Although he recorded the music, the thought of it makes him gag. Another time, he was forced to listen to a white rapper from a wealthy area record about how difficult life was "out here on these streets."

Brian was 19 years old, and Malcolm was only 15; Soy liked that they were young and hungry. The fact that they improved with each recording session made the transaction more sweeter. He was a businessman, after all, and they were his customers, but he was also a fan. He recalled Malcolm in particular as being incredibly inquisitive. He was curious about the functions of each item in the studio.

The meetings with Malcolm and Brian were enjoyable. They immediately realized that time was money in the recording studio, so they would write the songs together before going, then rapidly record them. The meetings went quickly, so they accomplished a lot of work. "He was a natural," Brian remarked. He didn't actually need to put forth a lot of effort. He would rarely alter the entire thing; he might retake it a couple of times, saying things like, "Oh, let me do another take." He simply moved on to the next.

They spent nine months in the studio starting in October 2007. The group's debut track was titled "Come Around." Anwar, the producer's name, was a Swede who Brian met through Myspace. Brian said, "He didn't believe in Mac." "I constantly engaged in combat with others. 'Yeah, I mean, you're cool, but what's up with this young dude?' others would say. 'No, this kid's dope, trust me,' I would say.

Chapter 6

Benjy Grinberg was graduating from the University of Pennsylvania in the early 2000s. Local Pittsburgher Benjy grew up in the same neighborhood as Malcolm's family, in Squirrel Hill.

Benjy had visited Israel about fifteen years prior. Benjy was only seven years old in 1985 when one of the children on the trip handed him a pair of headphones and said, "Check this out." A group of families from Pittsburgh had gone together. There was a Run-DMC song playing.

When Benjy turned up the hip-hop music on those trips home from practice, Artie would sit in the passenger seat of the Caravan, their heads bobbing in time. As they looked out the window at the bustling streets of the Steel City, Artie's thoughts would wander.

Some had existed. Tuffy Tuf's song "Ghetto Soundcheck" from 1991 had a modest hit, and Sam Sneed joined Death Row Records in 1994 and released the Dr. Dre-assisted song "U Better Recognize." Mel-Man, a producer and rapper, became friends with Dr. Dre and began rapping on his show, Dre Presents. Before joining the Doc's label as an internal producer, The Aftermath in 1996.

However, generally speaking, unlike earlier generations, the Pittsburgh rap movement had not given rise to many musical icons. It was a departure from custom because the city had a long history of music. Stephen Foster, a native of Lawrenceville who wrote the songs "Oh! Susanna," "Old Folks at Home," "Nelly Bly," and scores of other songs that many people today call racist, was widely regarded in the 1800s as the "father of American music."3 Dr. Frank Conrad aired one of the earliest musical transmissions over the radio from his Wilkinsburg garage in 1916, and Pittsburgh was home to KDKA, one of the first commercial radio stations in the world, which debuted in 1920.4 The Hill District was a hub for Black music and art from the early 1920s to the 1960s; nightclubs and ballrooms gave birth to jazz legends like Errol Garner, Mary Lou Williams, Art Blakey, and Earl Hines, among others.5 Later, Pittsburgh developed into a center for doo-wop, producing songs that are considered masterpieces in the genre such "Since I Don't Have You" by the Skyliners, "Come Go With Me" by the Del-Vikings, and—perhaps most notably—"Blue Moon" by the Marcels.

However, there existed a little underground rap scene that had not yet achieved much. Artie had that thinking while driving that day. Little did he realize that Benjy, his seatmate, appeared to be thinking the same thing as him. What could they do about it, though? They were still young.

Benjy shared a residence with his brother in New York and slept on his couch. He found employment with a company called Digital Club Network, which was founded in 1998 and specialized in webcasting concerts from locations across the nation, including the 9:30 Club in Washington, DC, the Great American Music Hall in San Francisco, and CBGB and Tramps in New York.

In its early years, the Digital Club Network amassed a substantial library of live performances, which were broadcast online through America Online in an era before YouTube. Benjy's main responsibility was persuading the performers to agree to contracts that would permit Digital Club Network to stream their performances. It wasn't a glamorous job. Webcasting technology was outdated, most people still connected to the Internet using dial-up modems, and the quality was poor due to the slow connection speeds. These weren't the times when musicians would hop into Instagram during the COVID-19 pandemic and play their whole discography outside on their balcony.

Being at Arista Records at the time was fantastic. When Clive Davis was replaced as president and CEO by Antonio "L.A." Reid in 2000, the corporation was under new management. Reid resembled a unicorn. He had a superb ear for talent and was a producer and songwriter. He could also function in the executive suite. His record company, LaFace Records, made stars out of Usher, Outkast, TLC, and many other artists in the 1990s. Two of his first signings at Arista, Avril Lavigne and Pink, had both achieved multi-platinum success. He was one of the most popular corporate CEOs.

Benjy served as L.A. Reid's right-hand guy for three years. He managed to swim despite being thrown in with the sharks. But since the music industry is predicated on hustling and entrepreneurship, Benjy seemed to think that in order to really grow, he would need to strike out on his own. In light of this, he made the decision to start his own label. He'd refer to it as Rostrum Records. A rostrum is a raised stage, or podium, upon which a speaker addresses an audience while standing. It was a suitable name for a record label.

So, in 2004, he signed Nitty, a rapper who wasn't actually from Pittsburgh. He actually came from the Bronx's Fort Apache neighborhood and traded in rap that was influenced by artists like MC Hammer, Tone Loc, and Will Smith. Which didn't stop him from scoring a minor hit that year with a song called "Nasty Girl," which was based on a sample of "Sugar, Sugar," a bubblegum pop tune purportedly performed by the fictitious rock band the Archies— as in the Archie comic books—and released back in 1969. At the time, it was a certified smash, reaching the top spot on the Billboard Hot 100.

It was unexpected that "Sugar, Sugar" became such a great success considering that the Archies weren't actually real. The song "just showed up," according to Andy Kim, one of the song's co writers, "the year of Woodstock, the year we landed on the moon, the year everyone was talking about Charles Manson and the Beatles were splitting up and they had that concert on the roof."12 Nobody gave the record any thought even at the time it was created. I had no idea what was going on, other than the fact that a lot of people were dismissing the song and the album as filler, he claimed. It was as if it had no significance and no worth.

It was hardly the stuff that produced legendary rap artists. But then, it didn't seem to be Nitty's intention anyhow. Nitty claimed in an interview with a music television program in Australia—where "Nasty Girl" had been enthusiastically received—that his goal was to just bring hip-hop back to its original joyous state. He aspired to be a "nice guy rapper, with lighthearted songs and videos."13 This music was designed to be mellow and, hopefully, move some units.

Benjy wants to locate some local talent though. He reasoned that since he was as connected as anyone and nobody from Pittsburgh had really achieved success yet, Rostrum should be the label to make it happen. Late in 2004, Benjy was listening to a mixtape produced by ID Labs, a small Pittsburgh recording studio that operated out of a storefront and published mixtapes with songs by the musicians who had recorded there.

The mixtape contained one song that drew Benjy's attention. He had never heard of the rapper before. His true name was Cameron Jibril Thomaz, but he changed it to Wisdom when he rapped, shortening the nickname his uncle had given him and adding the Arabic term for "leader." He thus assumed the name Wiz Khalifa.

Two years prior, Wiz had rather unluckily sauntered into ID Labs. He was fifteen years old at the time. When he was a baby, his military-employed parents got divorced, and he then spent a lot of his childhood moving around. He was born in North Dakota and has lived in states like Georgia, South Carolina, England, and Germany. However, he learnt how to record music and create beats using studio equipment that his father had bought when visiting him in Oklahoma.

Wiz was initially just another paying client at first. But E. Dan and another producer, Chad Glick, began to believe he had true star potential and wanted to develop it. As a result, they provided him with free studio time in exchange for a job answering phones and mopping floors.16

Wiz accepted their invitation. Which made sense given that the two were influential in Pittsburgh's emerging hip-hop scene. They had been a part of a group called Strict Flow in the late 1990s, along with rappers Masai Turner and MC Sied (who would later rebrand as Pittsburgh Slim and score a solo hit in 2007 with "Girls Kiss Girls"). The group was successful locally, selling cassettes for $5 each before releasing a twelve-inch single ("People on Lock") in 1999 through the New York-based independent label Raw Shack Productions. Although the record didn't make them famous, the group went on to tour locally and was frequently chosen as the opening act for acts like Nelly, Nas, Usher, The Roots, Jurassic 5, and Ja Rule. Without Further Ado, their debut album, was independently published in 2003.

They were kind of veterans and saw potential in Wiz, whose talent impressed them almost as much as how mature he appeared to be. Glick remarked, "He's got an old soul."17 They compared Wiz to rapper Nas, who established his name rapping lines like "When I was twelve, I went to hell for snuffin' Jesus," and who at the age of seventeen had appeared on the Main Source song "Live at the Barbecue."

Benjy signed Wiz Khalifa to Rostrum Records at the start of 2005. Wiz attended Taylor Allderdice High School and was a local youth. Wiz Khalifa was supposed to be the main artist for Rostrum. Wiz was prepared for it as well.

Arthur Pitt, a former basketball teammate of Benjy's, stepped in to help. Artie, who was eight years old when he went to Pittsburgh, was born in New Haven, Connecticut. He was born and raised in Point Breeze; his mother worked as a social worker and his father was a professor of pharmacology. After graduating from high school, he headed 90 miles north to Allegheny College with the goal of becoming a lawyer. He ended up studying history and creative writing there, though, and he also got into a ton of trouble.

The town where the school was located is known as Meadeville. It was fairly difficult. Really rural. There is a lot of countryside around. The zipper was first invented in Meadville. There used to be a zipper factory nearby, and I believe that when it failed, the town's economy also failed. Going to Perkins for supper was a huge deal even though it's more of a diner. I attended class and studied, but I also partied a lot. I had altercations. My parents gave me an old, broken-down Volvo during my first year so I could see my boys in Pittsburgh whenever I wanted to. I felt incredibly trapped up there. I was drinking excessively. I was simply incredibly bored in a little town. I was therefore detained. I eventually completed hundreds of hours of community service and was placed on college probation.

But in the end, Artie earned a degree with distinction. And after graduating from college, he moved back to Pittsburgh, where he was hired by a law company. He had a clerk job, which was low-maintenance yet offered him time to study for the LSAT. He might end up attending law school after all. However, he performed poorly on the exam, and the position proved to be fruitless.

When local journalists visited ID Labs during this time, Artie recalls them being blown away by the buzz surrounding Wiz and Rostrum. There hadn't been a Pittsburgh musician to get excited about in a while, but suddenly the local youngsters were on the verge of something.

Artie put Wiz on the front page of the Pittsburgh Post-Gazette in July 2005. Wiz would not only have a hit single and vanish, Benjy assured the newspaper; he would have a long career. People will love him and want to keep hearing what he has to say, much like Jay-Z or Nas, who may have 10 albums under their belts and still have people interested in what they have to say, according to him.

Artie had subsequently relocated to New York. He was dating his roommate at the time, and they both lived in Sunnyside, Queens. She distributed Wiz's songs among the staff of Warner Bros., where she worked in branding and marketing. If the label had heard of him at all, it was probably because of the press attention Artie secured for him. Wiz had received a lot of attention, especially on the websites of publications like Rolling Stone and XXL.

Warner Bros. was therefore intrigued. And the label sent Kenny "Tick" Salcido, an A&R scout, to check out Wiz's opening slot for Nas at Fitzgerald Field House in Pittsburgh in March 2007. That evening, Wiz approached the stage like a youthful veteran while wearing a black hoodie and baggy trousers and a Pirates cap. His slim body belied his heavy drawl as he crooned lines like "A dude grind, in due time, he's gonna blow / To make paper it takes patience, so walk it slow..." Wiz was also wearing a Pirates cap.

After watching their youthful leader destroy the place, the Rostrum gang was ecstatic. Tick appeared to be astounded by the spectacle. They went to a neighborhood bar to celebrate after the performance. Away from the college students and weekend warriors sipping their weak rum and Cokes, they purchased a few bottles and gathered in the VIP area. They raised a glass to their eventual success there.

Chapter 7

The Ill Spoken hustled alongside Rostrum Records in their effort to make Wiz a star. 48 tracks had been finished after 150 recording sessions when they set up camp in the studio.

The group started performing after their manager, Will Kalson, posted their music on the boards of RapMullet.com. The inaugural performance took place in 2007 at Moondog's, a blues joint in Blawnox, Pennsylvania, across the Allegheny River. Although it wasn't really the birthplace of hip-hop, they still put on the event and collaborated with other local musicians.

Malcolm was a natural performer. He had stage experience from his time with his previous bands, and he had an innate understanding of fundamental ideas.

The original dance fights between B-boys in park jams and neighborhood rec rooms, graffiti crews competing to bomb the most trains, neighborhood DJs trying to outdo one another with the loudest sound systems, and MCs spitting bars about one another at parties for neighborhood props all contributed to the centrality of beef in hip-hop culture.

Combat, beef, and rivalry were all a part of the hip-hop game. And whether it was KRS-One diss MC Shan on "The Bridge Is Over," Roxanne Shanté dissing UTFO to claim she was "The Real Roxanne," or even more recent fights like Jay-Z vs. Nas and 50 Cent vs. Ja Rule The unwritten rule of rap was that you couldn't back down when someone called you out.

The Ill Spoken started filling out their unofficial crew, the East End Empire, as they were working on How High. It was composed of local rappers, including Franchise, who was a rising star in Pittsburgh's burgeoning hip-hop scene in the middle of the 2000s. He came from Braddock, which is a suburb just south of upscale Point Breeze but feels like a world away.

Franchise didn't really stand out from the crowd in Braddock. He reasoned that hip-hop might be his ticket to a better life. In the early 2000s, he started recording songs with pals including Palermo Stone, Vinny Radio, and others. Franchise signed a contract with ID Labs at the same time that Wiz Khalifa started frequenting the facility. To keep it genuine, he remarked, "that was the thing that made me wanna go to ID Labs." "Wiz and another organization known as the Government were boiling at the time. I can hear how fantastic they sound. Although I don't want to sound or rhyme like them, I do want my trash to be as excellent as theirs.

Franchise would frequently scan the credits on mixtapes. E. Dan at ID Labs and a producer named Johnny Juliano who lived in the studio's basement were two names that kept coming up. He bought some beats from Juliano and started recording at ID shortly after. Because Juliano was so taken aback by what Franchise was producing on his beats, he started paying for them—sometimes for nothing or at the very least, at a discounted fee.

One evening, Franchise went to a club that had been converted from a sizable skating rink into a performance venue. "Wiz was headlining every Saturday for almost two months, with S Money and Chevy Woods serving as the openers. This particular time, I was outside after the club closed. I was handing out CDs of my mixtape, Perfect Storm, while perched on the roof of my girlfriend's car. A white child, who is little and short, appears. Franchise, I presume? Hey there, I'm Easy Mac. Hey, bro, I've been hearing your trash. I mess with your crap. I acknowledged that despite hearing about him, I had never met him.

Palermo Stone, who raps under the alias Tip Tha-Ill Spit, joined their group next and hung out with Vinny and Franchise.

According to Stone, there weren't many white rappers in Pittsburgh at the time. Franchise, on the other hand, was always admonishing me, saying, "Hey, there's this little white kid, man, you'd want fuck with him, he's actually very dope. I was given a performance one evening at a place called the Shadow Lounge. As I leave the performance, a cypher is in progress. The crowd is sizable. The cipher that is going off is being interrupted by someone. He's killing it, man. But I was unable to identify it. The crowd then dispersed. It's this little short-ass white dude, I see when I look. I asked him his name, and he replied, "Easy Mac."

Stone bonded with Malcolm and Brian almost as soon as Franchise and Vinny did. In addition to thinking they were cool youngsters, he also enjoyed their music. It was quite distinctive and very New York, according to Stone. "Everything was absolutely hip-hop authentic. They did make a sound.

People from distant places could listen to music created by relatively unknown children in Pittsburgh thanks to the Internet, but that didn't really signify anything. The Ill Spoken continued to work hard. But that was a beginning. And there was something there if you looked hard enough.

How High contains some of the distinctions between the two artists. Brian has a clean, precise flow, and his vocals pop against the beats. Malcolm also emanates assurance. He has a skillful way of delivering creative punchlines, which is an essential part of any rapper's toolkit. However, despite being present and clear, his voice is noticeably juvenile, full of air, and has the impaired breath control of someone who has smoked too many cigarettes.

Big L unfortunately passed away in 1999 after being shot nine times on a Harlem street corner. Although it may seem strange for Malcolm to have been influenced by Big L, he couldn't have chosen a better rapper because Big L had his moments. In his brief life, he left a huge mark on hip-hop culture.

Like in late February 1995, when he went to Manhattan's West Side from his residence in Harlem for a late-night freestyle performance on the Stretch Armstrong and Bobbito Show. He was joined in the studio by another MC, a man from Brooklyn, who announced when he got on the microphone that he had just left a club downtown that had been raided by shotgun-toting officers of the NYPD. The show was broadcast on Columbia University's radio station WKCR.

The two rappers that night freestyled for ten minutes, each spitting two verses. L appeared to sparkle the brightest. When he made his shrewd boasts, people's jaws fell because he was polished and exact.

Big L released his debut album, Lifestylez ov da Poor & Dangerous, the following month. The album, which was propelled by the songs "Put It On" and "M.V.P.," established him as a fiery lyricist who ranks among the finest in the business. The business was put on notice. After hearing Big L, Nas stated he was "scared to death." Nas had just released his historic debut, Illmatic. I can't possibly compete, Nas recalled thinking. "There's no way" if this is what I have to compete with.

Big L had the game in a chokehold back when being a lyricist meant something, and the most important tastemakers in hip-hop couldn't dispute that. He rapped with such fervor that his phrases made you stumble. Each verse was a magnificent composition. He was only on a different plane.

Although "Ebonics" wasn't a popular song, its originality and premise caught people's attention. L was ice-cold a few years ago;

now, business leaders were calling to close deals. One was a man he knew from Harlem named Damon Dash who later assisted Jay-Z in becoming a powerful musician. Together, they ran Roc-A-Fella Records, their own record label.

But Big L later passed away. That ended the matter. The producer Showbiz, who had worked closely with L, remarked, "We were all just stunned. "The world never even got to witness his entire range of skill. L was by himself in a lesson. It was simply insane.

More than just rapping over beats was required to be an MC. A true MC considered the art of rapping to be a distinct discipline. Rappers treated the art of rapping almost like a sport, honing their craft and taking it seriously. In the end, the distinction between a rapper and an MC was comparable to that between a cook and a chef with a Michelin star; the former used their skills to excel in their field, while the latter just serviced the public.

Malcolm aspired to be one of the best MCs, not just an MC. He was often so absorbed in it that he appeared possessed. Malcolm would sit alone in his bedroom on school nights, after the western Pennsylvania skies had grown gloomy, his parents had gone to bed, and the house had grown silent. He would scribble into a notebook, the crisp pages filling with rhyme after rhyme. Little did the child sleep. He hoped that one day his efforts would be rewarded.

However, Brian and Malcolm were also beginning two distinct phases of their lives. Malcolm was still in high school while Brian was saying welcome to his thirties. Heck, Brian dropped out of high school at seventeen and was now selling pot to pay his bills. He hadn't even completed his high school education. But at this point, Brian wanted to look back on that period of his life. He was committed to maturing and was focused. He also observed with disdain as Malcolm and his companions appeared to be following in his footsteps, which he later regretted.

However, he wished to free himself from their control. Malcolm said, "I really wanted to be independent." Therefore, he had options when he needed to quickly raise money to support his budding rap career. Like the time-honored custom of selling narcotics, which is practiced by everyone from Jay-Z to Jeezy.

He didn't have to do anything, yet he still made the decision to do it, which was highly privileged. He turned to Bill Niels, a buddy with whom he had since become close, to get help with this. The two would spend their afternoons at Bill's place smoking marijuana and killing time. Bill was an ambitious street pharmacist who, in his mind, would eventually supply Malcolm.

His warnings were meaningless. His friends would carry out their plans as planned. Malcolm also enjoyed hanging out with them. His parents disapproved, and there was occasionally tension at home. TreeJ was first prohibited from entering the building at all.

Brian had the same impression as TreeJ that Malcolm's parents weren't totally supportive of what was happening. He claimed, "I attempted to stay away from his parents at the time. "I'm sure I had a horrible reputation. Despite the fact that I doubtless had some positive influences. I made an effort to warn him about certain things. He had already made his own decisions, such as what he intended to do, though.

Even though his pals seemed unsightly, Malcolm found that being with them helped him a lot and referred to them as his "true inspiration." He claimed, "Those have been the same individuals who have pushed me ever since I [sic] just started." "When I announced that I was going to be a rapper, everyone just sort of laughed at me. There's no way this is going to happen, they said, not even listening to what I had to say. My friends, on the other hand, were the ones who stood by me and would ask, "Man, what are you talking about?" He is close.

Although he was actually a very bright young man, his performance at Winchester Thurston throughout his first two years was merely ordinary. Malcolm performed particularly well in courses that demanded genuine creativity, according to Pittsburgh City Paper interviewee John Maione, a performing arts educator who taught a course on electronic music production. He would bring listenable versions of his music for the other youngsters to analyze and analyze.

In the poem, he expresses his anticipation for the day when his family—who never seemed to be fans of him—will "finally drive me to insanity." Even yet, he calls himself "Hip-hop's child," drowning his emotions in melodies over beats while feeling lost and in misery. His neighborhood tells him that school is cool and drug users are thugs, and he feels so isolated that he can't bear to look in the mirror.

The poem has an underlying sense of discontent, disappointment, and feelings that are both irrational and persistent, not exactly the youthful anguish or the wrath that drives so many dreamers. In addition, it should be noted that Malcolm is being prepared for a particular kind of life, one that is well-intentioned and well-adjusted, in which he will develop into a responsible adult, attend school, find employment, get married, start a family, and possibly return to Point Breeze.

He wants more, though. Malcolm won't give up on hip-hop since it offers excitement, independence, and the ability to fulfill all of his boyhood fantasies. He wasn't buying into the alternative route that children in Point Breeze had taken ever since William Wilkins planted his roots.

His other objectives included using drugs and engaging in sexual activity, both of which were easier to do at Allderdice, a public high school that is referred to as "a melting pot for every neighborhood" in the city.

With the caveat that his grades didn't fall, he got away with a lot. However, they were in pain. college after graduating? Malcolm would be fortunate if he didn't simply quit school like his classmates did.

To make the gig, Brian took a flight from London, where he had temporarily gone to visit with a girlfriend who was studying there. It felt like true superstar shit, from writing songs in his mother's attic to

33

booking performances abroad. "I said, 'I'm cutting my trip to Europe, let's go! Atlanta via plane," Brian stated. It had a lot of power.

However, the show ended up being a lot of nothing. The performance, billed as a showcase, would expose Ill Spoken to Atlanta, which quickly emerged as the new hip-hop Mecca. However, no one in Atlanta knew who the Ill Spoken were. It was completely vacant, Brian recalls.

But the thing that sticks in people's minds about that evening is that Malcolm was supposed to have returned to the hotel by a specific hour. As the hour went on, his father was on it when he wasn't, blowing up Nelson's phone.

Even though the show was largely a failure, Malcolm's family seemed to have more faith in what he was doing the more things seemed to be going well for him. Who would they be if they didn't support his goals in a household where creativity kept the lights on and allowed the family to live a pleasant, decent life?

From rapping in his bedroom, his teenage kid was now being flown out of town for performances. No one showed up; not a huge deal. In any case, it was thrilling. Things were moving even though Malcolm's destination might not have been evident yet.

He consequently obtained employment at the Giant Eagle store in Squirrel Hill. He was to work as a cashier, a position that merely placed money in his pocket. It wasn't the hardest of occupations, but it wasn't the easiest either. Although it wouldn't make him wealthy, the job would teach him responsibility and how to be on time for work, preparing him for adulthood.

He spoke with the management before starting the job to determine his availability. How busy could a high school student possibly be? Malcolm informed the boss that he required flexibility. He would have to leave if he had anything to do with music. The boss informed him that wouldn't work; he could only work in cashiering or music. Malcolm reluctantly consented.

He was determined to report for duty on the first day that he was supposed to. But the more he thought about it, the less it seemed to make sense to him. The two would inevitably clash; furthermore, working at the grocery wasn't exactly his dream job. This was the exact opposite of what he planned to accomplish with his life; it wasn't what he wanted to do with it or what he was committed to do with it. He didn't have anything against cashiers; he just didn't like the practice.

He sent the manager an email just before he was scheduled to arrive to inform her that he would not be there. He believed he would leave before being let go. Malcolm was a rough, tenacious young man. He appeared to value and recognize the benefits of effort. However, he was unable to handle having an actual job.

MLK Mural was launched in 2002 as a community initiative by Wilkinsburg native Kyle Holbrook with the intention of keeping young children focused with art rather than harmful things. Murals could take weeks or even months to create, but once done, they would include jazzy flourishes and pops of vibrant colors that gave the city's public places a polished appearance. Street corners that would have once been populated by drug dealers and other types of inner-city stragglers were transformed into pieces of art in Wilkinsburg, East Liberty, McKeesport, and other places.

When he wasn't working to improve the perception of his hometown, Holbrook attended local events like Wiz Khalifa's Show and Prove album release party at the Brewhouse in Southside in December 2006, where he painted a mural in real time.29 Holbrook appeared to be the person who knew the town the best. Despite the fact that Malcolm was from a different neighborhood, Holbrook was still able to see that Malcolm had a distinct sense of ease about him and made quick friends with people he had only just met.

He was introduced to other budding rappers in the city thanks to the program, and some of them came to his home to record on the tiny microphone he had in his bedroom. It has occasionally been reversed, as with Paradise Gray. Gray had been a founding member of the Afrocentric hip-hop collective X-Clan as Paradise the

Architect in the late 1980s. In 1990, they released their seminal debut LP, To the East, Blackwards, to modest commercial success but later came to be regarded as one of the greatest hip-hop albums ever made. After relocating to Pittsburgh in 1992, Gray rose to prominence in the city by hosting the Pittsburgh Hip-Hop Awards and collaborating with the activist rapper Jasiri X33. When it came to the MLK Mural project, he appeared to have no qualms about inviting a young Malcolm, who was more than twenty years younger than him, to his home to record a song.

Eventually, the MLK Mural gig came to an end. Malcolm experienced the outcome he had hoped for. He joked, "That's what's really important in life, following what society says you should do. I did it for a little while to have a job and get on the right path towards what society tells me is the right path."

However, it appeared that his exploration of the city while posing as a painter exposed him to areas of Pittsburgh he might not have otherwise seen. In reality, despite Pittsburghers' claims to the contrary, a 2016 research found that the majority of white individuals felt this way about the city; those of color perceived it as being completely undiverse. Pittsburgh36 was named among the top five least diverse cities in the entire US by another research. In this city, both the demographics and neighborhood characteristics vary drastically over short periods of time.

Despite all of these early misadventures, Malcolm never wavered in his determination to realize his dream of becoming a rapper. But in order to truly become one, he had to first establish himself on his own, which was challenging given that he was a part of a group where he constantly felt outnumbered.

Malcolm, however, was adamant. He avoided conflict wherever possible. And being overruled? He could kind of live with that. Maybe in the end, the arguments simply increased his desire to act independently. But gradually, he started moving away. And instead of trying to split the group up amicably with a discussion about their disagreements, he allowed the music do the work for him.

There was no debate or conflict as the finale approached. No backstage explosion occurred, the sort of thing that Hollywood biopics and tell-all memoirs write about for maximum dramatic impact. The Ill Spoken never ever split up, in actuality. Brian and Malcolm both just jumped right into creating their own music.

He started by looking for a studio. Since Tuff Sound was the Ill Spoken base of operations, there was always Soy Sos, but a lot of the recordings Malcolm made there didn't seem to satisfy him. Soy Sos stated, "We created a few demos that were like, more sing-y stuff, guitar, things like that. But as a producer, "I didn't really have the tools to help him with the beats."

He intended to create a fresh mixtape. The Jukebox: Prelude to Class Clown is what he would call it. He hoped that if he did it correctly, it would bring him the kind of recognition that the Ill Spoken had never received. But he had to make one significant adjustment first.

Chapter 8

Malcolm had established himself by the time he was a junior in high school. He was the white kid rapping his little ass off at all the home parties.

Owner Brian Brick, who got his start in the neighborhood's hip-hop, punk, and graffiti scenes in the 1980s and 1990s, was encouraged when Malcolm brought in his first mixtapes. When Malcolm asked if Timebomb would promote it for him, Brian Brick responded, "Of course," he stated. Brick, he supposed, saw him as a "little clown."

Additionally, Malcolm and Brian had to contend with Pittsburgh's intense territoriality. At the time, no Pittsburgh rapper had ever achieved significant notoriety. Every young rapper was selling their own mixtapes, but the support was often severely constrained by the area you represented.

Malcolm couldn't even lay claim to a hood, which made matters worse. He was born and raised in Point Breeze, which on the surface didn't seem to be conducive to the stereotyped difficulties that many rappers at the time looked to be fleeing. He smoked marijuana and spent time with his buddies; they got into mischief, but he wasn't trying to get out of his dire financial situation. Malcolm was attempting to leave Point Breeze, the kind of community that hardworking people tried to enter.

In a genre where authenticity is valued (or was valued at the time), Malcolm's origins raised a unique set of problems. The only thing that made it worse was the fact that he was white. Despite the fact that there were other white rappers, his rather ordinary background made him stand out.

It was not surprising that Malcolm's credibility—or lack thereof—was a topic since hip-hop is Black music. Credibility, however, has always been a problem with hip-hop.

Concerns go all the way back to 1979, when the Sugarhill Gang released "Rapper's Delight," probably the first truly successful rap song. The Sugarhill Gang—Michael "Wonder Mike" Wright, Guy "Master Gee" O'Brien, and Henry "Big Bank Hank" Jackson—were actually just a group of guys hired by Sugar Hill Records executive Sylvia Robinson for the sole purpose of creating a rap song that the label could potentially cash in on. Despite being passed off as an approximation of the then-emerging hip-hop culture.

Big Bank Hank, who was a doorman at a Bronx nightclub and had previously worked as Grandmaster Caz of the Cold Crush Brothers' manager, further complicated matters by not actually being a rapper at all. Hip-hop lore claims that when under pressure to come up with words for the song, he stole some from Caz and mistook them for his own.

Hank passed away in 2014, and despite the other members of the band being upfront about it, he never admitted to stealing Caz's lyrics. "He didn't write the lyrics," Master Gee said to journalist Christopher Milan Thomas in 2006. He is a wonderful performer, really awesome at singing songs, and his voice is very elegant. He didn't write the lyrics, at least not directly. Where credit is due, it must be given.

This fact hasn't stopped anyone from playing "Rapper's Delight," though, and the argument is irrelevant because the song is a genuine classic. However, over time, this conflict between fact and fiction, real hip-hop and commercial rap, authentic vs inauthentic, would recur against a background where millions could be made overnight with the right song, the right look, the appropriate cosign, or affiliation.

Sometimes, concerns about an artist's past or ethics had little to no effect on them. Rick Ross' portrayal of himself as a sort of Miami drug lord may have been the most contentious, despite proof that he had previously served as a correctional officer (and was thus diametrically opposed to a drug lord). The hip-hop artist Akon gained popularity with his first number-one single, "Locked Up," and released a follow-up album named Konvicted, claiming to have served three years in prison for leading an auto theft ring. However, The Smoking Gun found that Akon had actually spent very little time behind bars. In fact, by the middle of the 2000s, hip-hop was so pervasive in popular culture that it seemed as though legitimacy and authenticity were irrelevant. Making hits was the only thing that mattered to an artist.

Which is not to say that fabrications couldn't have an impact on a career; it was difficult to sell lies, and for a white rapper, it was probably considerably harder. The truth might eventually come out if Malcolm pretended to be someone he wasn't; besides, it was exhausting. But if he stayed loyal to himself and found a way to demonstrate his gift, he would be okay. Few white rappers have achieved this delicate tango. On one hand, you could count them.

Similar to how the Beatles' appearance on The Ed Sullivan Show in 1964 spurred countless young people to establish rock bands, after the Beastie Boys' smash hit "(You Gotta) Fight for Your Right (to Party!)" white children across the nation appeared to start rapping. And record companies were more than happy to make room for them because they were hungry to make money. Simple enough, the objective was to sign the next great white hope and emulate what Russell Simmons and Rick Rubin had accomplished with the Beasties at Def Jam by signing him or her.

Then, in 1990, an intriguing event took place. One song started playing continuously on house stereos in the coziest, cutest suburbs as well as ghetto blasters in the toughest housing projects. Built around the opening bars of Queen's 1981 smash song "Under Pressure," it was a true earworm.

The song was named "Ice Ice Baby" and was unquestionably catchy. Because he was a white man, the musician who created the song went by the name Vanilla Ice.

With its success, "Ice Ice Baby" became the first rap song to reach number one on the Billboard Hot 100 (although the rock band Blondie technically beat Ice to the top spot way back in 1981 with their hit song "Rapture," which featured a rap by white lead singer

Debbie Harry, even though the song is not generally considered a hip-hop record). Vanilla Ice was then ready to remake rap—music and culture that are largely based on Black experience—in his white image.

Ice was rising to fame just like Hammer. He came off as amusing, amiable, and inoffensive. "The record company cleaned up my image, cleaned up my entire appearance, and then suddenly there's this good-looking kid out there, and they made it acceptable for the parents because they saw these kids dancing—oh, it's just a dance tune, it's now fine and let's find out who he is. Oh, he's good, wholesome, and all that," Ice said in a later interview.

At the time, Ice appeared to believe that by taking on the role of the face of rap music, he was not only promoting it but also had every right to do so. "I'm setting patterns here for other people to come along, bringing rap music into ears that have never heard it before or have never even considered buying rap music. And I'm white," added Ice. Because rap music is [Black], many people don't like that. Rap was invented by black people, but it also has its roots in the streets, which is where I come from.

His debut album To the Extreme* had more than two million copies sold by the end of 1990. Fans all across the world yearned to see Vanilla Ice live while "Ice Ice Baby," his hit song, was still playing nonstop on the radio. "A generation of suburbanites was captivated," Michael J. Mooney wrote in the Miami New Times.

In actuality, some aspects of Ice's biography were reliable. He used to alternate between Dallas and Miami when he was younger. He established a name for himself in Dallas by rapping and dancing at his manager Tommy Quon's City Lights nightclub. Although Ice was a bit of an outlier as the lone white lad in a predominately Black environment, the words to "Ice Ice Baby" were at least partially credited to another songwriter, Mario "Chocolate" Johnson. Ice continues to claim that he composed the song by himself, writing it in 30 minutes one evening in 1988. However, at the time, the song's genuine authorship and the boasts it contained only raised additional concerns. Perhaps Ice made everything up.

The words of Quon were ignored. This was America in the late 1980s and early 1990s, when it was still difficult to accept the idea of a white rapper. The crimes committed by former rock and roll celebrities were still recent. How the Beach Boys reportedly plagiarized Chuck Berry's "Sweet Little Sixteen" for "Surfin' U.S.A.," and how Elvis was named the King of Rock despite appearing to have drawn from the works of numerous Black performers who came before him. Hip-hop is becoming the sound of young America, much as rock once was. And Vanilla Ice gave off the impression of continuing tradition—another white man succeeding while the Black people who put forth the most effort were left behind.

The year 1991 saw Vanilla Ice's career pick up steam. He constantly toured, made two movies, and even started dating Madonna. However, the clamoring crowds and the persistent criticism that was directed at him proved to be too loud. He became irritated when he was accepting an award at the American Music Awards and retaliated, saying, "Those that try to hold the Ice Man down, can kiss my white ass."

He appeared on The Arsenio Hall Show the following evening. Arsenio's show was an outlier in late-night television; it featured rappers and celebrities that other presenters, notably Johnny Carson, who was still presenting The Tonight Show, were less inclined to book. A Tribe Called Quest or Ice-T sitting court on Arsenio's couch and lecturing America wasn't unusual on any given night. Arsenio acted as a sort of gatekeeper, so if Ice could gain the favor of his followers, that would be a major victory.

After a performance and a brief, mysterious appearance by Public Enemy member Flavor Flav—long before he became a reality television star, when Public Enemy was still recognized for its militant, politically charged music—Ice sits down on the couch while wearing a jeweled jumpsuit and has blonde streaks in his spiked hair. Arsenio asks him right away what he was referring to at the American Music Awards.

Ice said he is not interested in it and is unsure of what KRS-One meant. He continues by saying that some of his followers think that by introducing rap music to those who may not have otherwise heard it, he is assisting in its popularization. Rap music is here to stay, he claims, regardless of its color. "I'm not rap's Elvis. Vanilla Ice here. I'm not Elvis Presley at all.

Vanilla Ice was undoubtedly a legitimate star for a short while, but for all the wrong reasons. Vanilla Ice wasn't a popular choice. They simply adored a song he had written. He would only ever be a one-hit wonder, the answer to a trivia question about popular culture. He was high on drugs and drink for most of the 1990s; a cautionary tale. He had been gnawed up and spit out by the music industry.

But it was already too late. A white rapper would need to demonstrate great talent and exercise caution if they wanted to succeed in a post-Vanilla Ice world. Before embracing them, the media, the entertainment business, and the fans would have the rapper go through the fire. There wouldn't be a way to go back. Ice created a catastrophe in his path for white rappers.

In 1995, Wendy Day was scheduled to participate in a panel discussion at a music convention in Detroit. Day founded the nonprofit organization Rap Coalition, which assisted hip-hop musicians in navigating the frequently perplexing and occasionally unscrupulous music industry. She had collaborated with 2Pac and Chuck D, and years later she would become well-known for arranging Cash Money's $30 million agreement with Universal. She only realized that she was in Chicago when she should have been in Detroit on that particular day.

She therefore rented a car, accompanied by rapper Rhymefest (who later won a Grammy for co-writing "Jesus Walks" with Kanye West), and made the four- to five-hour trek without stopping to the D. In time for Wendy's panel, they arrived at the conference in the late afternoon. Day was ravenous because she hadn't eaten since leaving the Windy City. The idea was to move in the direction of a Denny's, which was close to the Atheneum hotel, where the conference was being held.

But a cypher was in progress when they left the venue. Rhymefest jumped right in, eager to establish himself. The day wasn't rushed. She had seen plenty of cyphers; they were frequently hit or miss. She was also quite hungry. She couldn't help but notice a man standing off to the side, not participating in the cypher but also not showing a lack of interest in it. She focused on Mark Kemp and they started conversing. She was informed of the local magazine he ran and the rapper he was collaborating with. The rapper in question appeared to be getting active in the cypher.

Day's next significant endeavor got underway at that point. She was going to assist this new white rapper in landing a deal. Marshall was his name. However, he went by the name Eminem.

Day was enjoying success as a figure in the music industry at the time. She assisted in the agreement that Chicago rapper Twista recently signed with Atlantic Records. She had a reputation for spotting talent in addition to knowing the ins and outs of the industry, how to negotiate contracts, and how to demand from companies what she thought the musicians deserved. The industry's lifeblood was new talent; executives built their careers on finding, nurturing, and breaking talent. Day was heated because she was assisting them with that.

It should have been easy for Eminem to sign a record deal. He had the talent, unlike Vanilla Ice, but he also had a past. His childhood had been particularly difficult growing up in Detroit close to 8 Mile Road. His family was chaotic and destitute, and his house was a mess. He experienced bullying in the mixed-race communities where he was raised. He left high school early. He had a daughter with a girlfriend he detested who had an on-and-off relationship with him.

Therefore, it came as no surprise that record labels were reluctant to sign another white rapper. When you could sign anyone in the world but a white rapper, why would you do that?

However, Day remained adamant. She recognized that Eminem was dedicated to demonstrating that he was among the best despite hip-hop growing more and more commercial, with dazzling videos and songs that might serve as advertisements for upscale items.

Battles were always crucial to Eminem since they were a part of his mission to establish himself as a brave MC. At the renowned Hip Hop Shop in Detroit, the 1997 Scribble Jam in Cincinnati, and the Rap Olympics later that year, he defeated numerous rivals. Eminem remarked, "Thank God for Wendy Day because she paid for my travel ticket. The timing was fortunate because he had recently been evicted from his Detroit home and had returned to find his goods scattered across the lawn and neighbors going through his belongings. It seemed as though winning that conflict would determine his entire future. "I needed that $500 because the first reward was $500. I lost. I was absolutely devastated.

However, the defeat turned out to be a blessing in disguise because Dean Geistlinger, a little child, was present. He begged Eminem for one of the tapes he was constantly giving out, and Em threw him one without giving it any thought. How many had he distributed so far? He must have spent hundreds of dollars, yet he had little to show for it. He was actually singing for his supper as he left the stage, and he wasn't even the winner. The EP he self-released on the tape was very different from Infinite, especially in terms of how violent he sounded. The method was the result of an alter ego he had developed for himself; through the ego, which was distinct from Marshall Mathers as a real person, he could rap about more sinister, disturbing, and violent topics like drug use and murder.

Dre appeared to care just that Eminem was talented. There it was. He was white, did that bother you? Without a doubt, there was no model for white rappers to adopt. Dre was also ice-cold in the business because he had failed with a compilation album (Dr. Dre Presents the Aftermath) and botched the production of The Firm's debut album (which featured Nas, Foxy Brown, AZ, and Cormega).

It would be controversial for one of the fathers of gangsta rap to collaborate with a white rapper, but controversy had advantages. Dre discovered that N.W.A's song "Fuck Tha Police" in the late 1980s angered the FBI, who mailed the group a letter objecting to the lyrics; later, worried parent groups pushed to have the song banned; and promoters sought to discourage the group from performing it. Which just increased N.W.A's notoriety and possibly increased record sales.

Then there came Snoop Dogg, his protege. Snoop had promise in 1993, but as his career was blossoming, he and his bodyguard were accused of first-degree murder in connection with the shooting death of gang member Philip Woldemariam. Even though he was ultimately exonerated of the charges, it wasn't before he used the negative publicity into the popular song "Murder Was the Case," which seemed to be inspired by the circumstances (and was later turned into an 18-minute short film with a soundtrack that ended up being the third best-selling record of 1994).

Finally, 2Pac was viewed by some as damaged goods, too loose of a cannon to take a chance on, after being shot, jailed on a rape accusation, and then involved in a personal conflict with the Notorious B.I.G., which started the East Coast vs. West Coast rap beef. But that didn't stop Dre (and then-partner Suge Knight) from releasing him from jail, signing him to Death Row Records, and producing "California Love," which quickly soared to the top of the charts (and stayed there for eight weeks) with its Mad Max-inspired music video playing on MTV almost nonstop.

Dre seems to be aware that where there was smoke, there was also fire. But in the end, Sam Goody couldn't sell headlines. Nothing Eminem achieved would have mattered if his albums weren't up to par, if he wasn't a legitimate MC, if all the shock and awe techniques he would later use to stir up controversy only ever amounted to controversy itself.

Malcolm wasn't Eminem or Vanilla Ice. Malcolm hadn't even been born when Ice first made his entrance into the rap scene. Malcolm, like many others, was an Eminem fan. He wasn't fixated on him, though.

The Marshall Mathers LP was an album that combined polished commentary with Eminem's signature shock and awe. While "The

Real Slim Shady" examines the media's double standards, "The Way I Am" touches on childhood angst and the Columbine school shooting, for which he, along with Marilyn Manson, received blame, "Kim," for example, finds our hero killing his significant other and stuffing her in the trunk of his car (not the first time he had rapped about that subject).

According to some estimates, the album may have sold 21 million copies. It was one of the best-selling records of all time in terms of sales. Malcolm was just eight years old when it was published, so even if Eminem's cultural influence was undeniable, it was unlikely to have had a lasting effect on him.

The one thing Eminem did offer was a chance. The music business was similar to other industries in that once something found success, others tried to duplicate it while making little changes. A door that had previously been closed was suddenly opened for white rappers.

White rapper Bubba Sparxxx, a Timbaland protege, was signed to Interscope Records, the same company that had launched Eminem's career. And just as Dr. Dre had given a white rapper a platform by endorsing him, Timbaland had done the same for Sparxxx.

A chopped-and-screwed mixtape, popularized by DJ Screw and, to a greater extent, his crew the Screwed Up Click, included commonplace components such cuts, scratches, and blends. But the music would be sped up to half speed and pitched down until the beats and words took on the appearance of an eerie, hypnotic drawl. Lean added to the effects, which were intoxicating.

Lean, often known as "syrup," "sizzurp," or "drank," has long been praised in southern hip-hop culture and was subsequently seen in the hands of singers like Lil Wayne and Future. Although the often catastrophic impacts of lean were hardly acknowledged, "Sippin' on Some Syrup," a Three 6 Mafia collaboration with UGK and Project Pat released in 1999, might as well have been labeled lean's unofficial anthem. In actuality, DJ Screw was discovered dead in his studio in November 2000 with an ice cream wrapper in his hand, despite all the work he had done to promote Screw music and lean.

Lean overdose combined with Valium and PCP was the root of the problem.39 He was only 29 years old.

The tragic death of Screw served as a lesson. However, it wasn't until seven years later that the tragic consequences of lean were publicly recognized. At that time, UGK's Pimp C, a true hip-hop legend who is best known for rapping on "Sippin' on Some Syrup," was discovered in his hotel room at the Mondrian. The 33-year-old was dead, kneeling on his bed in a stance of prayer and covered in blood.42 His unintentional overdose from lean combined with his pre-existing sleep apnea issue was blamed for his demise.

And while he couldn't deny the obvious—that Point Breeze was prosperous, liberal, and safe—and in some ways a throwback to the ideal of what an American neighborhood could be imagined by Norman Rockwell—he also couldn't ignore a peculiar aspect that Pittsburgh possessed: After a few blocks, that feeling of security vanished.

Malcolm was the first to admit as much. He said in an interview for MTV's "When I Was 17" that Point Breeze's convenient location led many to call it the "best neighborhood in Pittsburgh," putting him close to both luxurious homes and challenging housing projects. He was able to socialize with individuals from all walks of life as a result, not just wealthy or poor, white or black, but everyone.

He also has good taste in music. Malcolm has a broad, all-encompassing palate. He was equally knowledgeable about the music that many white people and Black people enjoyed. He was familiar with the songs that inebriated white people sung along to at karaoke, as well as the deep cuts that were played at the barbeque. Friends said he had a strong affinity for and intuitive understanding of Black culture.

The name stuck until he made contact with journalism student Quentin "Q" Cuff at Pittsburgh's Point Park University. Q kept himself busy when he wasn't studying by conducting rap artist interviews for the Globe, a student newspaper at Point Park

University, and Jenesis magazine, a local publication covering music and lifestyle.

One particular interview with the rapper Asher Roth, a white rapper from Morristown, Pennsylvania, who had emerged as one of the music industry's most promising new musicians, proved enlightening for Q. The Greenhouse Effect Vol. 1, a Gangsta Grillz mixtape he released in 2008, generated a lot of hype.

Malcolm and Q reconnected in the summer of 2008 at the Pittsburgh Indoor Sports Arena, where the Ill Spoken were opening for Soulja Boy. Malcolm thought Q had his pulse on things, so they decided to hang around. When they initially met, they spoke about life and listened to rap albums for hours on end. And from that point forward, Q would try to accomplish whatever Malcolm required.

And when Q started to get more involved, the subject of Malcolm's rap moniker came up again. Q believed he required a name with greater gravitas. Rappers began to see themselves more and more as brands. You needed a huge name in order to have a big brand. Malcolm's older brother's first name was Miller, and his maternal grandmother's maiden name was Miller. His grandfather had always called him Mac; it was a nickname. The more he combined the two terms, the more sense they made.

The Jukebox: Prelude to Class Clown was his first endeavor under the new identity. At ID Labs, where he first collaborated with engineer Josh Everette, he recorded the majority of the tunes. Malcolm had signed up as a paying customer at ID Labs like Wiz had done before him. He eventually convinced E. Dan and the team, though, that he had a little more going for him. The battles were one thing, but many of the young children in the Pittsburgh region looked to be enjoying the music.

In June of 2009, The Jukebox was released. Working along with Q, Kalson—who is still officially his manager—rented out the Shadow Lounge for the release party.

It became the place to be since everyone of all ages and genders was welcome. Mondays were jazz night, Tuesdays were "Steel City Poetry Jam," and another night was dedicated to a hip-hop open mic with a live band. We were all living it, from the staff to the other owners, said Strong. "There would be onstage cyphers where the bartenders would leave the bar and enter the stage. 'Yo hold my position, I'm on the open mic list next,' the doorman would say.

Strong was fourteen years older than Malcolm, and he preferred 90s hip-hop music personally. He added, "If it were up to me, I'd only be booking De La Soul and Camp Lo." However, despite the fact that the Shadow Lounge was mostly reserved for those over the age of 21, Malcolm was allowed entry despite his young age, which caused some embarrassing situations, such as the time Strong was "... yelling at him for having a bottle of Hennessy in the greenroom." But Strong saw that whenever Malcolm visited the Shadow Lounge, more guests appeared to arrive.

The Jukebox continued the musical theme from How High by the Ill Spoken. Without having to compete with his partner for attention, Mac was free to rhyme about anything he pleased, such as how his music defied classification. He raps, "I sound like old, I sound like new, I sound like me, I sound like you," on the song "Sound Like."

"Chow Line," an Ill Spoken song the group had released a year earlier and which Malcolm re-released because, well, why not?, features one of the hottest rappers in the streets at the time, Max B. Brian said that rapper Max B (who was shortly after given a 75-year prison term for conspiring to commit murder and robbery) "charged us a thousand dollars." At the time, he was awaiting trial. But it was worthwhile. He established trends. That undoubtedly gave us some traction.

The concept of the song's music video, which was directed by Ian Wolfson, who would later establish himself as Malcolm's go-to collaborator in his early videos, is straightforward: Malcolm is hanging out with Q when a girl walks by; he starts pursuing her, and the camera then follows them as they enjoy one other's company. Malcolm raps to her as he leads the group around town while she swings on a playground swing, her eyes blazing behind a red poncho. However, it turns out to be little more than a daydream when the female he saw ends up driving right by.

However, the studio was expensive. forty dollars an hour, three hundred dollars for a block of eight hours, and song-specific mixing costs ranging from seventy-five to one hundred fifty dollars. A single beat may be purchased for as low as $25, and 150 dollars could get you as many as 15 (three hundred dollars would buy you sixteen or more beats). It accumulated day after day. Malcolm's parents frequently paid the bill.

Malcolm and his friends occasionally carried out fraud to pay for the studio. For the money, Stone claimed that "we were doing a lot of stupid sh*t." "TreeJ would offer this white youngster fake marijuana. similar to oregano in a bag. He would bill him after packaging one ounce. We attempted to take crap to the studio by pawning it or by attending home parties and stealing it. like a flat-screen TV we stumbled upon at a gathering. When the kids throw a party while the parents are gone, we simply go there, pee, and leave. Since their parents were unaware that they were hosting a party, they were unable to inform them. We would be in the back trying to get some stuff off so we could get some studio time while Mac would just be rapping and bullshitting because he had such fantastic energy.

Malcolm, however, was prepared to pay. He paid Jerm to sample "Just My Imagination (Running Away with Me)," the Temptations' number-one single from 1971, since he was determined to turn it into his own fantasy. Malcolm raps over Jerm's soulful beat about his idealized version of life, which includes a king-size bed, a swarm of women, clothes, jewelry, money, cars, mansions, and more. In other words, it has all the makings of a typical aspirational rap song. However, for Malcolm, the song acts as a sort of audio vision board; this is what he imagined for himself and would eventually have if he kept working.

Josh Everette had been involved in a vehicle accident by the time Jerm took over the main engineering tasks at ID Labs, therefore the majority of the recording work for Malcolm's sessions fell to him.

Malcolm would arrive at work with his raps already written because money was limited.

He would quickly record the tracks he demoed at ID Labs. He did not overthink his own creations when he was alone. He was only focused on getting the job done. Malcolm remarked, "I like to be able to capture it shortly after I compose it. "Because when you first write a verse, you're never as excited about it."

And day after day, he would isolate himself in the studio, a modestly sized, unremarkable structure that, according to some estimates, was no larger than 700 square feet. The studio's back room served as the "A" room, where Jerm would arrive in the evenings to start his sessions and keep them going until the early hours of the morning. E. Dan worked out of the "A" room during the day. Although it wasn't particularly elegant, the location was adequate.

Malcolm was also making an impression on Jerm, who recognized qualities in him that E. Dan had once recognized in Wiz Khalifa. "There was a charisma, just a natural kind of thing," Jerm remarked. "Wiz and Malcolm didn't need to exert themselves too much. Likewise, work ethic. Many folks wanted to record their one song and create a video back in Pittsburgh. Even when they were younger, the two treated it more like a career.

The fate of another artist who was making waves overseas at the same time as Malcolm was honing his skill and transforming himself from Easy Mac, a man who just loved to rap, into Mac Miller, a more serious artist, would have the most impact on his nascent career.

Chapter 9

Rostrum Records believed it had achieved success. Warner Bros. had had enough even though Wiz Khalifa's hype hadn't quite reached a fever pitch. Wiz and Warner agreed to a contract in June 2007, with Rostrum overseeing and acting as the production business.

Warner had high hopes for Wiz. A&R rep Tick, who signed him, was encountered by a music executive at a trade show. The executive had recently secured a deal at Warner for Jean Grae, a singer he represented. Tick was someone he wanted to involve.

Therefore, it was understandable why Nas had just said that "hip-hop is dead." However, Wiz appeared to have a different self-perception. He believed he could have a significant impact if given the chance. Rostrum didn't stake everything on him just so he may become a viral sensation and then vanish. So after releasing the hit song "Youngin on His Grind," he released the mixtape Prince of the City 2.

On the mixtape, Wiz is still finding his voice and his feet; he shouts out parts of his rhymes with a stylised focus, appearing to be a touch unsure of who he is. But there are advantages. He sounds at ease in other tunes. a state of comfort. He improvises a reflexive "Uh-huh," which is on the verge of becoming his hallmark. The rhymes are aggressive, with an East Coast accent, and the beats are bottom-heavy and Southern in bounce. One gets the impression from Prince of the City 2 that Wiz is from both everywhere and nowhere. He is an unadulterated talent looking for a sound to call his own.

The popular single and mixtape served as appetizers to prime listeners for the main course, a proper single called "Say Yeah," which was released in 2008 and sampled Alice Deejay's "Better Off Alone," a Eurotrance hit that had seen success in everything from upscale dance clubs to weddings and Carnival cruises.

No matter how well the song did, it wasn't sufficient. Warner, who had earlier been ecstatic about Wiz, was now cautious. Wiz desired to have a major label album released. Wiz remained in the studio, which had now been transformed into ID Labs by Rostrum. Warner, however, refused to approve the project.

Wiz quit Warner Bros., Rostrum reported on July 16, 2009. In a press release, they cited Warner's persistent postponements of the release of Wiz's debut album while also promising impending independent projects from him, such as a mixtape with the rapper Curren$y from New Orleans titled How Fly and a cross-country tour set to start in the fall of 2019.

The New Music Cartel, a group of music websites that included NahRight, 2DOPEBOYZ, OnSMASH, YouHeardThatNew, Xclusives Zone, DaJaz1, and MissInfo, was responsible for breaking a lot of new music in the hip-hop genre. Although there were others, these were the top sources for hip-hop music. You may listen to the newest music every day, not just from well-known performers like Lil Wayne or Kanye West, but also from mid-career musicians like Cam'ron and undiscovered artists like Sean Price.

Benjy was contacted by a little, New York-based label called iHipHop as things began to heat up. Known for its efforts in the underground hip-hop scene, Babygrande Records' sister business, Jedi Mind Tricks, Hi-Tek, and several other random Wu-Tang members all had music in its library. The purpose of the new enterprise iHipHop, run by Chuck Wilson, was to market "cool" music.

Wiz has long been a favorite of Ruddy's. He radiated an energy that was intangible. Ruddy compared him to Snoop Dogg for the younger generation. He consistently had a joint in his mouth. You know, you'd never really see him sad, and he never really expresses it in his music. He was a cool-ass motherfucker, so I guess it was simply a matter of relatability at the moment. He had the Doggystyle appeal for young ni**as.

Ruddy attended Wiz's concert at the Williamsburg, Brooklyn, waterfront in the summer of 2009. Fans knew every word to Wiz's songs, which were only accessible on mixtapes, and the concert was crowded, and Wiz tore the place up.

The argument for releasing an album was straightforward: blogs assisted in the discovery of musicians, yet blogs had limitations. Despite the fact that certain artists were also being [pigeonholed] as blog artists, Ruddy noted that "artists were propelling from the blogs." Wiz would receive more than just a day's worth of mentions on all the blogs with a good record; he would receive marketing, promotion, PR, the works. iHipHop allegedly made Rostrum an offer for a deal that would have cost $50,000.

Deal or No Deal is an album that Wiz published via iHipHop on November 24, 2009. He celebrated it with a performance at New York's Highline Ballroom, which was hosted by blogger Combat Jack and radio broadcaster Angela Yee.

It helped that the album was jam-packed with hit songs, many of which exhibited the effortless calm that Wiz's fans and Ruddy alike found so alluring. Wiz was surrounded by a frenetic energy and buzz. This young man had potential. Everyone was able to perceive, hear, and feel it.

Malcolm was stuck in high school in Pittsburgh while Wiz Khalifa was taking stages in New York.

He published his first entry on listentomac.blogspot.com on October 15, 2009, explaining that he had started the site to update his followers: He wrote, "Go tell your friends!" It begins, "Yours Truly, Mac Miller."

It was not a novel concept for an artist to write their own blog articles and address their followers or anyone else who happened to visit their website. Prodigy, a member of the Mobb Deep, operated an honest and occasionally amusing blog at HNIC2.com while he was incarcerated, while Kanye West was known to publish images and rants on his website KanyeUniversity.com that were very similar to the ones for which he would eventually become renowned.

He wasted no time in getting the promotion. A day later, he posted the following entry, which was a leak from the next mixtape he was producing. The mixtape was titled The High Life, and the single was titled "Pen Game". It included popular underground rapper Skyzoo from Brooklyn and was shared across all sites; Malcolm made sure to thank 2DOPEBOYZ for helping him get the single heard.

However, it didn't seem like anyone really cared to publish his music until he had a song starring someone of greater notoriety, someone whose music was routinely put on the blogs—like Skyzoo. Early on, he began to understand that he had a game to play. It all came down to who you were standing next to in the music business.

Another important question was about college. He was in his senior year of high school and, if he attended college at all, he planned to graduate and join Nomi at Temple. See, while Asher Roth was preoccupied extolling the virtues of college, Malcolm pondered whether the whole experience might be exaggerated. He toured colleges and performed at some of them. He frequently left feeling unpersuaded.

In October 2009, Malcolm's top priority was The High Life, a mixtape he believed would attract the kind of exposure that may put him in a far better position. not just a young person rapping on the internet to gain popularity. not just the students at the neighborhood high school. Not only a youngster who could perform admirably at local colleges. If being signed on the dotted line wasn't his major objective, it was the one thing he had always craved: respect.

He didn't lack direction, but at the end of that month, he appeared depressed and desperately wanted to leave the narrow world he seemed to live in. In Pittsburgh, he claimed, there was nothing for people his age to do, which was restricting. He had grown tired of clubs and bars by the time he was seventeen. In his letter, he stated, "I'm not hating; I'm just looking for something greater for the next couple of years of my life. "I desire to journey. not only to NYC, but also to other nations. Until I can say that I have traveled the world, I won't feel that my life is complete. Let's hope that transpires.

On December 16, 2009, The High Life was made available, just a few weeks before Wiz Khalifa's appearance at the Highline Ballroom. Even though it had only been a few months after Malcolm's prior release, he had made significant progress.

His mastery of social media had a role in how quickly he was adopted by listeners. He made it a point to be present wherever people congregated, whether it was on Myspace, Facebook, or

Ustream. These platforms were more than just opportunities to promote himself; they allowed him to express himself in a distinctive way. He posted all of his video footage on TreeJTV and joined Twitter early, where he quickly racked up followers.

However, booking shows required a team effort, so in addition to Q, there was Will Kalson. At Indiana University, he was still enrolled, and he was a part of a network of college promoters that organized performances for students who spent their weekends juggling red Solo cups. These kids were constantly looking for fresh methods to release their pent-up energy. They also adored Malcolm.

One of the performances Kalson landed was at Indiana University's Little 500, a week of celebrations, performances, and unrestrained revelry that annually takes over Bloomington's streets. In 2009, Wiz, DJ Unk, and Young Jeezy were scheduled to perform; Malcolm was added as the opening act, and he rallied his pals to make the seven-hour trek from Pittsburgh to Indiana.

Mac believed that his performance couldn't be topped as he exited the stage. It was slain by him. destroyed the building. We likely performed one of our best gigs ever, according to Stone. "But when Wiz finally appeared, he stole the stage by shittin' while standing atop speakers. Mac probably realized we had to work harder as a result.

The music video for the jazzy song "Live Free," for which the graphics were recorded during a brief trip to New York City with his team, captures some of Malcolm's wide-eyed exuberance. The gangly trio of old friends—Malcolm, TreeJay, Q, and Bill Niels— can be seen leaving Penn Station and heading east to Chinatown while stopping at bars and admiring the city's beautiful lights. The world beyond Pittsburgh is shown to them as they journey.

The song and the music video for "Live Free" gave off a carefree vibe, but there were some limitations to the good vibes: at the time, some of Malcolm's pals started experimenting with more original means of being free.

When Wiz's mixtape Kush & Orange Juice was released in April to widespread praise and became a hot topic on Twitter, Rostrum was enjoying its own popularity. At the time, accomplishing this feat was uncommon.28 Malcolm had no doubt noticed this and was considering his options. A record deal was the typical path for any aspiring performer. Wiz was a local artist, and Rostrum was a local label. Rostrum was undoubtedly feeling the energy at that particular time.

Yet Malcolm was exploring other possibilities. He had already become friends with Darrelle Revis, a cornerback for the New York Jets who is older than Malcolm and was a star at Pittsburgh before moving to Pennsylvania.

Revis enjoyed singing and playing the drums in his leisure time, but he had just started his NFL career and had no genuine music industry expertise. He had some money, which he used to pay for some of Malcolm's studio sessions—a total of less than five grand. One of the sessions even resulted in a collaboration with Revis under the name Mr. Manhattan that was named "Friday Night Lights" and was motivated by the house party scene in Pittsburgh.

Malcolm was banking on Revis to open some real doors for him while Fleming turned his newfound interest in Mac Miller into a legitimate website—MacMiller.org—complete with message boards where youngsters could discuss his new crap. He had already started working on a new project after The High Life—a mixtape he believed would represent his age. He believed strongly that the work would produce favorable results, including bigger events and perhaps even a legitimate record deal.

Revis and Geiger believed they had struck gold. And they scheduled a meeting for Malcolm at Sony Music for the first part of the 2010 summer. A Tribe Called Quest was famously signed to Jive Records by Barry Weiss twenty years previously, and Mac was a major admirer of the group; he had "Beats, Rhymes, and Life" tattooed on his forearm. Weiss is one of the most accomplished executives in the music business. Weiss had dealt with white rappers before; during his hip-hop career, he signed a contract with a lesser-known Kid

Rock. He now occupied a position of authority as the company's chairman and had the authority to immediately sign Malcolm. Malcolm's life could have drastically changed in an instant, just like Revis did when waiting for his name to be called at the NFL draft.

Malcolm was thrilled at the chance. It wasn't so much about the money a record deal may bring in as it was about the opportunity to have his art, which he worked so hard to perfect, be seen by more people.

Malcolm and his friends then drove from Pittsburgh to New York to attend the meeting. He met with Revis outside Sony to talk tactics. They intended to leave the meeting having reached an agreement. Revis compared it to playing baseball and how an agent may convince a player they were competing for a large payday. You held your hopes high, but you had no idea if you would succeed.

Sony ultimately declined Malcolm's request. They never explicitly expressed a lack of interest in him, but he could read subtle cues. That particular day, he left the meeting with his head hung low.

He and his team huddled once again with Revis outside the label. With book bags strapped to their backs, a group of young children watched the activity around them. Malcolm was curious as to what would happen next. Unofficial assistant Revis informed him that he wasn't really sure.

The following month, KIDS decreased. Then it exploded.

Chapter 10

When Malcolm McCormick was in the eighth grade, he saw Kids. The cinema verité aspect of the movie, which captured young people in downtown New York City at their most insane without any Hollywood phoniness, intrigued him.

To that goal, the characters in the film drink, skateboard, smoke, and fuck. Malcolm had the impression of looking around and asking,

"Aren't I doing the same things as my friends?" They weren't quite as extreme; they weren't raping virgins and spreading HIV, as in the movie's conclusion; they weren't even chasing virgins. Even if they aren't the same thing, hanging around and getting into mischief felt very comparable.

There was some validity to the idea. His fan following was expanding thus far, but he hadn't yet made a striking declaration. He was able to rap, as The High Life demonstrated. But he needed to accomplish something definite, something distinctive, in order to really establish himself. There were emerging rappers everywhere. Many were skilled rappers. That was insufficient.

He started to picture a project that had the vitality of children poured into it. Of course, music and movies were different mediums, and Malcolm felt that his generation, raised on Harry Potter and Lord of the Rings, Outkast and Jay-Z, Mean Girls and Freaky Friday, The Hills, Laguna Beach, Paris Hilton, Kim Kardashian, Jersey Shore, The Sopranos, Entourage, Curb Your Enthusiasm, Myspace, Facebook, and Twitter, as well as a lot of Internet porn and mime, was superior to that of the kids in Kids because they It occasionally seemed hollow that they had been told from birth to follow their dreams. They would eventually have to accept an entirely typical life, just like everyone else. How miserable.
But as soon as Malcolm was out of school, he started considering his next steps. It was definitely not college. He was beginning to receive payment for gigs, and his music career had gained enormous pace. It began to seem more like a job than a passion to make music. There was still plenty to demonstrate. And he kept returning to Kids as he worked in the studio that summer.

Hip-hop had not yet experienced a contemporary youth movement until that point. Teenage rappers were more inclined to crank that Soulja Boy, show you how to dougie, or teach you how to swag surf if they were seen. Older musicians were still concerned with the accouterments of the previous hip-hop music industry: cash, glamor, and glamour. It sometimes seemed as though these artists were from other planets in the Internet era.

Many fans enjoyed boom bap hip-hop's throwback atmosphere because it wasn't trendy; others, however, were turned off and expressed their disapproval by making disparaging remarks on Twitter about how distasteful the music sounded. Who was this little child, a white child no less, mocking a genuine hip-hop masterpiece created by a man who received little to no notice from the general public while purporting to own the beat? The fact that many blogs who posted the video neglected to identify Finesse—their authors were probably too young to have understood who Finesse was—didn't help matters.

It didn't really matter in the end. There wasn't any backlash because this was just how things were at the time, and the video was receiving hundreds of millions of views. The industry would undoubtedly pay heed now if they hadn't before.

Malcolm took his knowledge of hip-hop culture very seriously. He frequently devoted hours to searching through old YouTube videos in quest of ideas. His older brother and pals also helped him by educating him on music from earlier times. The videos appeared simplistic because that is what they were.

Rostrum had come a long way by that point. Even though they were still an independent label, they had big plans. After his performance at the Highline Ballroom in 2009, Wiz was hotter than he had ever been, and Atlantic Records' Zvi Edelman wanted to sign him. It would mean a return to the majors for Wiz and Rostrum, but on different conditions. Nothing false, not a single deal.

Regardless of whether Malcolm wanted to sign with Rostrum, the label had to gain the approval of Mac's mother before anything could be accomplished. Although there was potential for the business, Karen supposedly had reservations, as any mother would. He had been hanging out with those guys for years: TreeJ, Will, and Q. However, a group of senior males stood out.

Malcolm's friends said that the offer was a 360 deal. It was common for labels to support an artist's career in exchange for a portion of everything—record sales, merchandise, endorsements, and touring income—during the Motown era, which gave rise to the 360 agreement. 360-degree agreements fell out of favor for a long time because people believed they were bad for the artist. However, they became more prevalent in the early 2000s when smaller, more nimble independent labels started to take on the labor-intensive tasks that major labels had handled, including marketing, public relations, and tour support (and the related financial load).

The contract had a 360 structure in addition to having little to no advance payment. When Malcolm signed the contract, it would not have cost him more than $1,000, according to him.

Bill Niels can still vividly recall that day. The photographer Larry Clark, who directed the film Kids, first rose to fame with the photo album Tulsa, which chronicled his friends' drug use. Bill was inspired to take up photography and would take images of Malcolm and their pals whenever he could. He didn't give it a second thought; it was just something to do.

The acronym KIDS means for Kickin Incredibly Dope Shit; after all, the mixtape's purpose was to showcase Malcolm's rapidly developing rap abilities. Malcolm's life was exciting and joyous at the time, thus the content reflects this. Prodigy, a Mobb Deep rapper noted for saying that he "put his lifetime in between the paper's lines,"15 was doing exactly what Malcolm was.

But even as KIDS spends a lot of time having fun, it also includes some intimate moments. The song "Poppy," in which Malcolm tells his grandfather Milton "Mickey" Weiss all the things he wishes he could have said, is very significant: Only twenty-four hours had passed since his grandfather's passing when he wrote the song.

He had to hold back tears while he recorded his voice for "Poppy" at the recording studio. Malcolm was always the joyful kid, grinning and cracking jokes; no one at ID Labs had ever seen him this way.

No matter how challenging the workouts were, Malcolm never lost his composure. He was certain that KIDS would result in something good. The same as with Ustream, the more he gave out, the more he received in return, and consequently, the more his movement expanded. The secret was to simply keep going; to seek assistance when necessary—that was what Rostrum was for—but to avoid depending on anyone else to bring about his future. Being a fly on the wall during the meetings gave you the impression that history was being written.

"Knock Knock" was the tune that truly made it happen. The song, which is based on Linda Scott's top ten smash "I've Told Every Little Star," flips the original's AM radio-style production and turns it into a fast-paced banger—West Side Story meets Westside Connection. It was created during one of Malcolm's initial sessions with producer/engineer E. Dan, who had joined the project as a result of Rostrum's capacity to compensate him on a per-project basis. Malcolm discovered the sample, brought it into the studio, and E. Dan started composing a rhythm around it right away.

Malcolm, however, was adamant. They left New York at eleven o'clock that night, pushing Malcolm's Honda Civic west on what Artie and Benjy used to call the "suicide drive," a 400-mile journey over a wide expanse of American emptiness so boring it felt like death. Will Kalson was the driver.

Once Malcolm was back in Statik's Brooklyn basement, the idea was to record a song with Termanology, a gritty MC with a difficult flow. Statik immediately called Malcolm after learning that he was a fan and instructed him to travel from his home in Lawrenceville, Massachusetts, where he resided. However, Statik remembered that Term was reticent. The trip took four hours. Additionally, he was unaware of Mac Miller. Statik assured him, "Trust me, bro, this kid is gonna blow up." So Term got in the car and started heading south. While waiting for both rappers, Statik engaged in conversation with a visiting XXL magazine editor named Rob Markman.

Statik claims Markman informed him that Malcolm was not hot enough to make the magazine's annual Freshman Class list. Although Statik claimed Malcolm would, he was mistaken.

Malcolm then showed up. And shortly after him came Term. Once more, Term grew reticent. The two began rhyming after Statik turned on the instrumental of "Paid in Full" by Eric B. and Rakim. Malcolm wasn't what Term had anticipated—he wasn't simply some white kid who had somehow made himself look hot on the Internet, but a real dope.

Even though Rostrum was now participating in the release of KIDS, Malcolm still believed it was important for his "day ones"—those who had helped him from the start—to hear it first. So, on the day of the release, August 13, 2010, he went on Ustream, the platform that had previously served him well, and teased the impending release.

KIDS was broadcast live to the public. The initiative quickly drew praise from Malcolm's devoted followers. It was a warm welcome to Mac Miller's world for people who were unfamiliar with him. Infused with the vivacious energy of a recluse stoner raised on hip-hop from the 1990s, modern music, and indie rock, KIDS is steeped in old-school charm. It sounds like the mixtape was created by the young person who was always skipping class to get high with his friends. It seems appropriate that it happened soon after his high school graduation. Malcolm put everything he had into KIDS because it was his chance to succeed.

Malcolm's race was at least largely to blame for the hatred. Aside from Wiz, Pittsburgh didn't really have a hip-hop scene, and he was from Pittsburgh. And there wasn't a cosign; working with Wiz and sharing a label with him made people take notice, and he acknowledged that their collaboration, "Cruise Control," had given him much-needed exposure23. However, their relationship wasn't like that of Dr. Dre and Eminem, where it seemed like one artist was completely under the other's wing.

Even so, there was more love than hate, and Malcolm had the chance to witness both when he visited New York for a press tour the week after the release of KIDS. A party was held that Monday, August 16, at Sway, a Moroccan-themed SoHo bar that New York magazine had deemed "the definitive late-nineties lounge."24 Still popular in the aughts, it gained popularity again with its Morrissey-themed Sunday night parties. It was the kind of club Lindsay Lohan would occasionally drop by for a guest DJ set and where relatively unknown musicians, such as a young Lady Gaga, would have to request to have their albums played.

Artie and his friends had to wait outside since they were too young when Malcolm and Artie arrived at Sway. The location was small; it could accommodate 200 people. But that evening, it was full. In fact, it was so crowded that some of Malcolm's rivals were also present. Malcolm was positioned next to Team Facelift, who were sitting on a couch against a wall near to the DJ booth. Team Facelift was a group that Time Out New York previously referred to as "endearing white-dork rappers," and included future Internet celebrity the Fat Jew.

Malcolm was bothering Team Facelift so much that one of them grabbed a drink and hurled it at him. Malcolm merely sat there dumbfounded for a little period of time as the drink missed. Even though he wasn't old enough to purchase a drink, other white rappers were throwing them towards him.

He simply knew that at two in the morning, he would grab the microphone and carry out his intended mission. That evening, not many individuals in the crowd were familiar with him. But it seemed like these were the kids that the movie Kids was really about fifteen years after its release. Malcolm had now joined them right there.

The most crucial aspect was that none of it reached him. He grinned through it all, regardless of the drink that was thrown in his direction, the fact that his boys were turned away, or the confused throng that didn't know what to make of a teenager who appeared to be lost while attempting to find the Chinatown bus back to the suburbs.

Chapter 11

With excellent intentions, the Blue Slide Park access road was built. Malcolm has been traveling and releasing music for about a year. After the release of KIDS, there was a frenzy of activity that lasted until the beginning of 2011, when he started his first significant tour, the Incredibly Dope Tour.

Anything Mac Miller accomplished, whether it was a song, a video, a performance, a tweet, or anything else, made him move more quickly. His engine was the fans. They listened intently to everything he said, as if he were giving the Sermon on the Mount. He was also simply being himself.

Every night the gigs were sold out as they made their way from California through Oregon, across the coast into British Columbia, back through Washington, Utah, Colorado, the Southwest, the Midwest, and ultimately Pennsylvania for a close-out performance at Club 27 in Philadelphia.

But traveling was exhausting. The speed was constant. You spent one night in a city and left the following morning; all you did in between was drive.

Behind the scenes, he was anything but the cocky, swagger-oozing rap star he tried so hard to project onstage. Will Kalson remembered that "He would get really nervous before shows." "I recall him having to take a shit or throw up before the event early on, for sure. That's a little disgusting, but he'd get tense. He merely wanted to perform well. He wanted everyone to be content. And he really took that seriously.

But despite how difficult the journey was and how far he was from Nomi, who was enrolled once more at Philadelphia's Temple University, Malcolm did like it. He was eager to please the girls who were swarming at him. A female in the audience once claimed to be hurt at a concert in Minnesota; when the EMTs arrived and carried her backstage, she leaped off the stretcher and went onto the stage to grab him.

He had been working toward the concerts, parties, and fans all along. Moving on to the next show, each one is a tiny improvement over the previous. What a contrast to his previous existence in Pittsburgh, when he shared a run-down apartment in South Oakland's rent of $1,300 with TreeJ, Bill Niels, and Q.

The dream was of this. The others around him were aware of it. Bill Niels remarked, "It was arguably the best winter of Mac's life.

However, some adjustments started to be made inside Malcolm's inner circle at this same time. Malcolm had seen Q as his manager ever since he had first met him. He traveled a lot with TreeJ and Will Kalson; they served as his "team." However, Rostrum was now having a bigger impact because it was both a record label and a management firm.

There was an inherent conflict of interest when an artist signed with a company that served as both a manager and label; what was best for the artist wasn't always what was best for the label, and vice versa. Additionally, the management would essentially be acting against its own interests, so the artist wouldn't have someone on their side when issues arose. On paper, the arrangement didn't make much sense, but it was and is still common.

Malcolm exhibited a tendency to concur. He would have likely signed the contract as soon as it was placed in front of him because he had always wanted to be on Rostrum, but he took his time because he had people in his corner raising questions about the deal and, more especially, whether Benjy was the ideal person to lead his career. The contract remained unsigned for months. Rostrum, to its credit, continued to work for him.

Malcolm has the makings of a future major star, according to XXL. He appeared to be already on his way, and Rostrum was one of the hottest new labels in the business, along with Top Dawg Entertainment, which is home to Jay Rock and Kendrick Lamar. Most significantly, Malcolm's music was beloved by the XXL staff. "Some white kid from Pittsburgh doing boom bap rap stuff—his shit was catered to the nineties," remarked Rondell Conway, a former editor. "However, it was his allure. His tale was that. I love my hometown of Brooklyn, but I'm realistic about hip-hop. That style of music was being performed by a different person. I was learning about Mac's childhood in Pittsburgh rather than in Queens, Staten Island, or the Bronx. Consequently, it had an additional layer. Musically, I could relate to it, but what he was saying was novel to me. I had never heard this rendition before, and I thought it was fantastic.

Thus, XXL chose him. Along with Kendrick Lamar, Lil B, Meek Mill, YG, Big K.R.I.T., Cyhi The Prynce, Lil Twist, YelaWolf, Fred the Godson, and Diggy Simmons, he was there at Industria in NYC filming the XXL cover. "Lil B was probably the biggest star at the time, and his energy in the room was huge—Mac was the only person who could match that energy and buzz," recalled Conway. Now, if you walk into a room full of rappers, they're all tough and on guard. Mac, though, didn't have a pretentious attitude like, "I've got to be a rapper, I've got to be the star in the room, and not talk to anyone." He would talk to anyone, whether you were a member of the staff, the guy getting the coffee, the woman pressing clothes, or the woman applying makeup. He was simply genuine.

Malcolm was expected to become a star, and as with every Freshman Cover, XXL's reputation was on the line. And he was now influencing other musicians who may potentially become stars in the future. Artie was aware that this would advance Malcolm's professional standing. But he was surprised when the Rostrum deal came up right after the filming.

Artie acknowledged that five albums was a lot of music, but the ball was finally moving in the right direction. Malcolm informed him that he would sign nevertheless. Then he simply stopped. at least not right away. Rostrum was satisfied to leave things as they were because "Black and Yellow," Wiz's first significant hit song, was rising the charts and serving as the Steelers' fight song as they advanced to the Super Bowl. They were one of the most popular music labels. Malcolm is a fool if he allows them to do all of this work without signing.

It was difficult to resist getting caught up in the excitement of it all with the entire Most Dope group onstage. Bigwigs from all the major labels were also dispersed among the children, anxious to find out what all the commotion was about. Some appeared to be completely convinced, such as Republic Records President Avery Lipman, who Artie reported as declaring that Mac Miller was "the future of music." Karen was beaming as she observed her kid succeed in the Big Apple from the balcony.

Fun was had. Even though it was work, it didn't feel like work. He conducted interviews and photo shoots for the press for twelve hours prior to the concert, and although clearly exhausted, he never voiced any complaints. After the event, there was more publicity; he had to do interviews, handshakes, smile for this person, take their picture, and remember the supporters. But this was the end. Malcolm had agreed to this upon signing up. He was now actively playing. The moment has come to play ball.

In his hotel room that evening, at one in the morning on March 11, 2011, with Benjy by his side, Malcolm signed a contract with Rostrum Records. As he had done with KIDS, he went on Ustream to give his followers the URL to his upcoming mixtape, Best Day Ever, which was set to drop later that day. "Everyone who's been here since the beginning; whoever has been here since Mackin Ain't Easy, since The Jukebox, since The High Life, since KIDS, since yesterday, since this Ustream—basically, everyone—I want to thank you guys, we're making history tonight, for real," he said, holding a Corona in his hand. I recall having five viewers when I did Ustreams. There are 20,000 people present. It's quite bizarre.

The song "I'll Be There," which is dedicated to his mother, is also noteworthy. He raps, "See, I was six years old with a dream, when my moms told me I could do anything," over a sweet piano riff. Phonte Coleman provides a guest vocal on it. One of the rare musicians who can claim to be one of your favorite rapper's favorite rappers, Phonte was a member of the North Carolina duo Little Brother and is still regarded as a cult icon today.

However, one song on Best Day Ever stood out as being a step beyond the rest. It was distinct from other things in its bop. After a nine-hour train voyage from his home in Delaware, the producer, named Sap, arrived at ID Labs one evening. He entered the studio and discovered Malcolm at the computer, smoking and sipping

Hennessy. Sap opened his laptop right away and began browsing through samples. One piqued Malcolm's attention.

Malcolm didn't pause to consider it at the time. Real estate tycoon Donald Trump turned his success into a reality TV program called The Apprentice. Rappers adored Trump because he was extremely wealthy and not ashamed to display it. Malcolm wasn't even the first rapper at the time to write a song on Donald Trump; Big Sean also did it.

The song was so popular that some DJs decided to play it even though it was never pushed to radio. It entered the Hot 100 at number 75, which is a respectable ranking for an independent record in the era before streaming services were common. When the video's sixteen millionth watch occurred in July of that year, Trump started tweeting about Malcolm and the song.

Not all of his buddies were as fortunate. Bill Niels stayed back when the crew left because he didn't really have much to do. He started selling narcotics because he needed to pay his rent. The home was also deserted. He started doing drugs since he had nothing to actually keep him busy. Years of dabbling were followed by a period of intense effort. Malcolm wasn't on board. not initially, at least.

It was for leisure purposes. And it was difficult to resist narcotics while driving. Whatever place Malcolm landed in, there was always some sort of party favor to partake in. Statik Selektah met him at a Massachusetts after-party and inquired about his plans. When Malcolm revealed that he had been sniffing cocaine and taking pills, he was taken aback.

Malcolm's curiosity ultimately prevailed. Bun remarked, "You can already see that's what he had in mind and that's what he was going to accomplish. "He and his crew had it in mind that they would want to test the syrup when they arrived in Houston. Like, the majority of visitors to LA want to smoke continuously. There is really no way to necessarily talk folks out of that experience because that is just a part of it. Similar to when your parents advise you not to do something, even if you hear them and understand what they mean, if you are determined to carry it out, you will do it when they are not present. You'll conceal that behavior.

He gave the album the name Blue Slide Park. It was given that name after a place he frequented as a kid close to his house. In a metaphorical sense, it represented a little area of Frick Park; the further into the woods one went, the more things they uncovered. He wants that vibe for the album. The park, though, stood in for his life.

Additionally, the record's joyful, carefree, and youthful tone was intended to reflect the idea. According to ID Labs producer E. Dan, "He's really focused on the idea of keeping this fun." He says things like, "Let's keep it a playground" or "Make it more of a playground."

The mob devoured it. He played all of his mixtape cuts. He played a number of Blue Slide Park tracks. He jammed on the guitar in the middle, playing Weezer, 2Pac, and Oasis songs. After saying "thank you" to his parents, he sang "Poppy," breaking down in tears at the conclusion. When he ended with "Donald Trump," everyone lost it.

Chapter 12

Malcolm was grieving. The final performance of the Blue Slide Park Tour was scheduled for December 8th. He had previously performed there at Stage AE as Wiz Khalifa's opener. Then, he was met with jeers and boos. The teenage rapper had not yet entirely won over the crowd.

Now that he was returned, he was a different man and artist. Then came KIDS, followed by videos that received millions of views on YouTube, Best Day Ever, "Donald Trump," the EP On and On and Beyond, the mixtape I Love Life, Thank You, and—even better—more than 200 performances and the number-one album Blue Slide Park.

If only they had known the journey he had made months previously to HeadQCourterz, the former location of D&D Studios in New York, in order to consult with DJ Premier, the famed producer who had worked on records there with many of the rappers Malcolm admired.

The Premier affirmed that he could and then left. He reasoned that Malcolm would be watching TV in the living room when he got back. But five minutes, ten minutes, fifteen minutes later, he returned to the studio and saw Malcolm standing in the booth where he had been left off, enveloped in total darkness.

As the man pursues his aspirations, Malcolm can be heard describing a dialogue with a woman—likely Nomi and him—in the song. Critics could have praised it for its insight if it had been performed by another rapper, but they struggled to accept Malcolm's saccharine ode. It could have easily fit on any pop playlist.

Even yet, he was able to comprehend the slights. "On one of Blue Slide Park's tracks, titled "Up All Night," he simply keeps drinking: drink, drink, drink, drink, drink. Reynolds remarked, "It's some shit about drinking. "That song alone definitely contributed to his inclusion in that frat group. Additionally, he was white.

It seems that his skin tone was only a small component of the issue. Being white in hip-hop was one thing, but fully embracing it was quite another.

In retrospect, Pitchfork's Sargent stated, "Asher Roth had his one hit around the time Blue Slide Park came out—I wanna say maybe a year or year and a half prior. I believe that at the time, my interest in it was sparked by the thought that "frat rap" was a genre that was truly taking off.

Prior to Blue Slide Park, Sargent didn't know Malcolm all that well. However, he found it difficult to reconcile the LP's economic success with what he perceived to be its egregious mediocrity. It had to be the fact that he was a white man peddling subpar white rap to ignorant white children. Because of that, knocking him down a peg was practically a form of social justice.

Regardless, Malcolm smelled bad after reading the Pitchfork article. Prior to that, Malcolm had mostly been allowed to go about his business as a random American white person, free to go and do as he pleased. He had endured difficulties, yes, but nothing like having the world's most reputable music publication question his basic existence.

The review has something else added to it. An issue that surfaced one evening when Malcolm was waiting for Blue Slide Park to release and Benjy was driving, long before the Pitchfork review had been released.
Malcolm ended the year well by performing alongside Demi Lovato, Selena Gomez, Jason Derulo, and J. Cole at an MTV concert that was broadcast nationwide on New Year's Eve.

The song, which was well-liked, discussed Malcolm's potential advantages from having faith in his own ideas. Making something out of "The 900 Number" seemed too absurd to warrant real effort when he was writing the song at ID Labs.

He might appear to be sitting alone at first glance. Features weren't present in Blue Slide Park, Best Day Ever, or KIDS. On the mixtape I Love Life, Thank You, he started working with additional people, including Sir Michael Rocks of the Cool Kids, Bun B, and Talib Kweli (who he met through Clockwork, a former DJ for Kweli's band Reflection Eternal).

He would write some of his most moving lyrics to date on soulful songs like "Family First" (with Kweli), in which he addressed his detractors, went into detail about his problems with Nomi, and commented on the growing distance he was experiencing from his family. The rapper raps, "It's hard when I can't even find the time to call my mom / And she thinks I'm goin' Hollywood, I guess she probably should..."

He wanted to cooperate on Macadelic with a similar spirit, but in a way that seemed true to him as a person. It wasn't as tough to control the guests as he had anticipated. While on the Incredibly Dope Tour, he met Juicy J for a night of partying at a California studio;9 He met Cam'ron in New York after traveling to Harlem one night at three in the morning to see the Big L mural on the corner of 140th Street and Lenox Avenue (which later inspired a collection of songs they hoped to release as a Step Brothers-themed project). He talked to Kendrick Lamar, another XXL Freshman, "all the time," and they met in person.

But much to Malcolm's astonishment, he soon received a response from email: YMCMB, Malcolm recalled. He discovered the complete recording session when he opened the email. The only issue was that Malcolm couldn't tell what the music sounded like because there wasn't a final version of it. Instead, he had to open each file in Garageband individually and mix the music down by himself. Hearing Lil Wayne's unprocessed vocals, in his words, was "surreal."

One of Macadelic's notable songs is "The Question," which poses existential questions that individuals may face whether they are working in an office cubicle somewhere considerably less interesting or famous rappers touring from state to state to play for boisterous crowds.

Both the music choice and the lyrics matured along with it; Macadelic is rife with drug references and the entire CD has the vibe of having been produced while high. He raps, "I got codeine in my cup!" on the song "Loud." Another song, "Vitamins," has him high on LSD or mushrooms and experiencing a psychedelic adventure.

Malcolm did make a change when he became Macadelic. The mixtape was a gamble for the musician who had established himself as a bit of an optimist (he had a signature "thumbs up" motion that he frequently used in music videos and photos), as it was direct and violent with several references to drugs and booze. Yes, this was Malcolm, but he was now older and far more irritable.

He was fully aware of himself in every way. KIDS was all about goals and ambitions, what he aspired to achieve; Best Day Ever reflected his excitement now that he had accomplished some of what he had set out to do; and Blue Slide Park was motivated by his love for home, according to him in a 2012 interview with Hard Knock TV.

However, it was only a minor portion of a growing backlash against not only Mac Miller but also white rappers in general, as Malcolm's ascent was, if anything, merely a byproduct of a wider movement. In a post-Asher Roth world, the rap game was overrun with white rappers, including YelaWolf, RiFF RAFF, Action Bronson, Machine Gun Kelly, G-Eazy, Macklemore, Iggy Azalea, Hoodie Allen, and Ricky Hil (the son of fashion designer Tommy Hilfiger). Some people were having success, whether they were independent or signed to majors.

It's possible that Kreayshawn, a tattooed white woman wearing bangles, was the white rapper who started so much of the criticism. Her song "Gucci Gucci" had gone viral that summer and earned her a million-dollar record deal with Columbia Records. The song was a smash that people seemed to appreciate, therefore the early excitement was justified. But shortly after it went viral, Kreayshawn was hounded by controversy when it emerged that she had used the

N-word in several of her tweets. Although she admitted her error, she justified her use of the word by saying that she had grown up in Oakland, California, where she claimed people of all colors used it.

If white guilt wasn't bringing him down, it was the performances' poor attendance and inability to fill the stadiums. He was downhearted.

Finesse argued that Malcolm's career had begun with "Kool Aid and Frozen Pizza" and that it couldn't have happened without his beat. It was difficult to argue against that. The song "Kool Aid and Frozen Pizza" had about 25 million YouTube views at the time of the lawsuit, and KIDS had almost a million streams and downloads. Even though it wasn't the only thing that ignited Malcolm's career, it undoubtedly did.

Finesse finally made an attempt to speak with Rostrum. The song wasn't being sold by the label, but Malcolm was singing it, and those appearances were bringing in money that Finesse was not. He probably would have felt differently if he had received credit and payment. Finesse claims that when he finally made contact with Rostrum, they advised him to see the situation as though Malcolm had done him a favor.

Malcolm didn't budge. Because the Oscar Peterson sample used in "Hip 2 Da Game" had never really been approved, he believed Finesse had no legal standing to make a claim. Other than that, though, it wasn't as though he had verbatim copied the song.

But more than just money was on the line. Rappers would frequently, if not always, rap over already-existing instrumentals without ever being sued. Finesse countered, though, that there were restrictions on what might be done with an already-made instrument. He believed that Malcolm had merely rapped over the track and presented it as his own, adding nothing special to it.

The press had a field day while waiting for the court to decide where the line between tribute and blatant stealing was established.

Malcolm, a white rapper who previously battled the idea that he was a culture vulture, received yet another setback.

In the end, Malcolm was dissatisfied with the litigation. He had always admired musicians and producers from the 1990s. In his own way, however misguided it may have been, he believed that by adapting their music and rapping over it, he was bringing old-school hip-hop into the 21st century in the same way that musicians from the 1990s claimed they had done by sampling musicians from earlier generations—and facing legal repercussions as a result.

The problem: too lean. Lean was syrup; it contained only sugar and caused weight gain. People started making remarks about that as well, labeling him a drug user. He also retweeted those messages.

Rostrum was nonetheless worried. Finally, a tour with Mac Miller and Wiz Khalifa was ready to start. The tour, dubbed the Under the Influence Tour, would also include Chiddy Bang and a budding Compton rapper by the name of Kendrick Lamar. There could be 20,000 people in the crowds. This was a significant step up, so Malcolm needed to be at his best.

A series of conference calls between Rostrum, Mac's parents, and the investors in the label then started. The topic: Malcolm's slack language.

The label suggested that he be removed from the tour; alternatively, they debated whether it would be wiser to retain him there while also adding a life coach.

But stopping a train in the middle of the track was challenging. In addition, nobody seemed to be able to communicate with him.

Chapter 13

Amidst a frenzy of tour dates and his burgeoning interest in drugs, Malcolm came to Los Angeles in the spring of 2012 to film an episode of the MTV program Punk'd.

The secret to success for an independent artist in the Internet era was action. Activity implied focus. Buzz meant being focused.

His work covered a wide range between collaborations, mixtape cuts, and authorized remixes. He collaborated on tracks in 2012 with legendary hip-hop artists including Raekwon the Chef, Fabolous, De La Soul, and Talib Kweli, as well as up-and-comers like Meek Mill, French Montana, and Big Sean, Rostrum Records musicians Wiz Khalifa and Boaz, and Curren$y and the Cool Kids from the blogosphere. Even Justin Bieber wanted him to be on a remix because he was that good-looking.

One initiative, though, seemed to gain precedence over the others in this bustle of activity. Pink Slime was the name of a collaboration EP that was solely produced by Pharrell Williams.

Ten songs were produced during the recording sessions, which began in Miami around the time Blue Slide Park was released. Malcolm had collaborated with a few well-known producers, like Just Blaze, DJ Premier, and Jazzy Jeff, but Pharrell was unique.

Eventually, the tracks "Onaroll" and "Glow" were released. They were powerful performances in which Malcolm, in a lighthearted manner, addressed the important issues at hand, including the Lord Finesse lawsuit, his newfound rich status, and his weight increase.

He also used other methods to declare his independence. On the Under the Influence Tour that summer, an event on the opening night in Atlanta highlighted how far apart he had become from the label.

Artie claimed that his mother had discovered Malcolm with lean while she was backstage at the performance. Artie was informed as a result of her pulling him aside, and after he fled, he discovered Mac cowering behind his security guard.

The person who almost discovered Malcolm, who assisted in getting his music on important websites when few people were aware of him, and who worked for him pro bono until Rostrum signed him, was now being treated like any other label employee. However, the Under the Influence Tour wasn't given that name by accident. Everyone, from the performers to the audience, appeared to be buzzed.

A.D. Amorosi stated after the tour's stop in Philadelphia, "Though the precise number of barfing, swooning kids wasn't quantified, this reviewer hadn't witnessed vomiting like this since Bridesmaids."

But compared to what was occurring behind the scenes, what was happening in the public was insignificant. Malcolm had a significant issue. He was totally dependent on lean.

Malcolm's close collaborator remembers attempting to get in the studio with him in the autumn of 2012. But Malcolm begged off, saying he had to return to the east for a reason. The producer thought he was going to rehab, but he was unable to confirm it.

While it's unclear if Malcolm ever did actually check himself into treatment at that time, his songs may offer some insights into his thoughts. In the song "These Days (Dope Awprah)," which he posted to SoundCloud in October 2012, he sings: "What the fuck happened to that sweet kid / That you knew when he released that mixtape called KIDS... I believe I should visit a doctor.

He first tried quitting his cold turkey habit in order to get healthier. That wasn't going to help him because he would just wind up binging. He eventually succeeded in moving lean to the side, albeit he never acknowledged how he did it.

He needed to lose weight quickly because he would soon be on national television. MTV has backed Malcolm almost from the beginning of his career. He had won the Woodie of the Year Award at the 2012 mtvU Woodie Awards, had an appearance at the network's prestigious Video Music Awards, and made cameos on shows like Guy Code and Hip-Hop Squares. It seemed as though MTV News was following his every move.

Malcolm had only recently moved to Los Angeles, but MTV executives thought he was already living the dream of every young man. He was recently famous and lived in the City of Angels with his wild pals in a big-ass house. This was the ideal scenario for a reality television show, a genre that MTV practically developed 20 years prior.

But for years, he had been uploading behind-the-scenes recordings on YouTube. His friends were in the vids, and they were kind of intriguing. Jimmy was a creative of some sort; Q was his straight-laced manager; Clockwork was his music-obsessed DJ; Peanut, a late addition to his group, was his fashion-obsessed merchandise designer; Big Dave was a huge and hilarious former NFL lineman who served as Malcolm's bodyguard. The show may make sense if he could include his friends.

YouTube videos produced by musicians or their record labels were nevertheless low-risk. No big deal if no one watched online. It was significant when a network invested funds in a real production and hired a crew to film, edit, and sell advertising alongside it. It was also a gamble.

Malcolm acted as the globe around which everything else revolved. Rob and Big served as the show's model. That program, which followed the exploits of Rob Dyrdek and his pal Big, had been a smash success for MTV. Malcolm may be like Dyrdek, according to the network, and his pals would be like his Big. The program, billed as a "docu-follow," focused more on giving viewers a glimpse into Malcolm's daily life than it did on drama.

Even though it wasn't written, episodes were loosely timed to events in Malcolm's life. He was scheduled to receive Complex magazine's Man of Next Year award, thus that incident turned into an episode. Larry Fisherman and Larry Lovestein were his alter identities, and those turned into episodes. Going home became an episode since Pittsburgh had such a significant role in his life.

The entire situation had devolved into a catastrophe. Ahmed was prompted by it. In the course of his career, he spoke with a lot of rappers and famous people. Most tasks went without a hitch. not this one though. Although he had a good relationship with Malcolm, he wasn't sure how he would feel about giving him a gift that didn't work. Not only did it not work, but it also appeared to provide a genuine risk. The car wouldn't have been the only item to blow up if he had a different disposition.

Malcolm and Donald Trump had only had a passing familiarity up until that point. Trump appreciated that Malcolm had the song named in his honor. The fact that Trump put his name on everything that could be made or sold, including steaks, skyscrapers, and clothes, has transformed narcissism into an extreme sport. However, Trump wasn't lounging about listening to rap music. Anything that looked to increase the value of his name made him happy.

Trump had spent the most of a year claiming that Barack Obama wasn't born in the United States and was, therefore, unable to be president. He was no longer a playful and entertaining person. "Show us your birth certificate," he commanded. The birtherism movement was just getting started at the time. He was considering entering the presidential race himself.

He was all the while winning over a vengeful and resentful segment of the right-wing political establishment. When Malcolm wrote the song, they were the last things on his mind.

Later in his career, Malcolm would debut other personas, but Lovestein served as a welcome distraction, replete with a self-produced EP titled You by Larry Lovestein & The Velvet Revival, a made-up band with its own Twitter account and just him as its sole member. Although anyone made aware of its existence would only be aware of it because it was created by Mac Miller, the alter ego allowed him to create another genre of music that was precious to him—jazz—without the expectations of it being released by Mac Miller.

Although in episode four, "PA Nights," he returns to Pittsburgh for his mother's birthday dinner and does make an inadvertent joke about cocaine, the show avoided anything that was too harrowing for television.

Chapter 14

Home to the entourage is Hollywood. It is also about sprawl, more so than in New York, where space is at a premium. The wealthy and famous can and frequently do live in comically large homes with more space than is necessary, so those spaces get filled with family, friends, and whoever else is temporarily deemed essential. However, the city is otherwise gritty and appears more glamorous on television than it actually is.

Malcolm resided in one of those homes, a mansion actually. He was unlike so many of the prominent people in town since he maintained a lax policy with the door, more MTV Cribs than Airbnb. You only needed to know him or know someone who knew him in order to gain access.

The studio, a windowless room that smelled like menthol cigarettes and had red walls and red lighting, was a prominent component of the home. It was called "The Sanctuary" by Malcolm. Malcolm remarked, "It appeared to be an opium den." He presided in the studio as he worked on numerous projects. One of them was a brand-new album.

The new album continued the direction he had started with Macadelic, which was more inward-focused and ornery, as opposed to Blue Slide Park's festive and enjoyable nature.

Malcolm had developed. He was aware of it. All those around him followed suit. It was all fun and games two years ago. He was visiting a new city each night as he traveled the globe. But the relentless work had a price. Additionally, fame had worn him out.

But his explanation didn't seem to make sense. Malcolm and Ahmed spent the night in the studio together. Nothing appeared to have changed as I observed him at work. He may have kicked Lean. He continued to indulge nonetheless. "Weed and alcohol are not the same as other drugs, but usually when people are in sobriety or are going through rehab and stuff, they kick everything, even stopping drinking coffee," said Ahmed.

That evening, Malcolm wasn't by himself in the studio. Earl Sweatshirt had unexpectedly arrived carrying a six-pack of beer and a bottle of Knob Creek, and MTV cameras were there. The atmosphere was initially strained. Earl's location at the Coral Reef Academy in Samoa, where his mother had put him to keep him out of trouble, were made public by Complex a year earlier. He became one of the most talked-about musicians due to the mystery surrounding his absence from Odd Future during the band's peak, which resulted in a Free Earl movement and an adoring 8,000-word piece in the New Yorker.

Earl recently responded in "Chum," rapping: "Craven and these Complex fuck ni**as done track me down / just to be the guys that did it, like, "I like attention."" Complex had revealed all of that. Earl and a Complex representative were now slated to speak in person. The encounter might have been explosive, but nothing actually transpired. Any remaining bad vibes were immediately extinguished, and business as usual got started. Ahmed then noticed a curious phenomenon.

Earl emerged as one of Malcolm's better pals among the many people that passed by his home. Odd Future was known for generally detesting everything, and just the way they spelled their name—Odd Future Wolf Gang Kill Them All—seemed to contradict almost everything Malcolm stood for. Kill people, burn crap, and fuck school was their remedy! But they managed to compromise.

Another partnership started that same month. Not the drinking party that gave birth to "Guild" or any of the looseies that seemed to sneak their way onto the Internet, it appeared to come from another universe. It was improbable that this song would be discussed in the rap blog comments or dissected on a hip-hop message board.

A young woman who had performed in the Broadway play 13 at the age of only fifteen and then landed a supporting role as Cat Valentine in the Nickelodeon television series Victorious—which, after four seasons, had just aired its series finale—performed the song, "The Way," and was something of a child star. Like Malcolm and numerous other teen pop stars before her, she amassed a devoted fan base by posting cover songs to YouTube and keeping an open social media presence.

Ariana Grande was her name. She was also enormous in her own right. Ariana was a native of Boca Raton, Florida, and Victorious was a popular program that received millions of viewers each week. Her on-screen persona, Cat Valentine, was a fan favorite and cheerful Pollyanna.

Ariana frequently performed on Victorious cast CDs and occasionally dueted with Victoria Justice, but in secret, she was working on her own music with the hopes of breaking out on her own. She began working on what she anticipated would be her debut album in 2010. In 2011, Monte Lipman signed her to Universal Republic after receiving some of her YouTube videos.

Friends who were around him at the time recall that Malcolm was acting in ways that to them seemed a little out of character when it came to Ariana. Maybe they were, or maybe they just weren't as familiar with him as they thought they were. For instance, in November 2012, Ariana was playing the role of Snow White in the Pasadena Playhouse production of A Snow White Christmas. On the day in question, Malcolm asked Clockwork whether he wanted to go with him after accepting her invitation to attend the performance.

Clockwork was absolutely unaware of Ariana Grande and had no idea who she was, but he remembered the play as being "super dope," and after it had ended, he remembered waiting for Ariana to leave the theater with Malcolm. He had been on the road with Malcolm for two years by that point, and he appeared to think he was fairly well-known and well-known. However, while he waited outside with Malcolm, he noticed that the photographers were swarming the location and completely ignoring his friend.

Ariana did not like the paparazzi or how she was viewed by them. She was a singer who initially rose to fame as an actor; she was a child star who, at the age of 20, was transitioning into adulthood. She wished she could have been so much more than she already was.

However, "The Way" was actually their first joint appearance. The song was Ariana's first single off her debut album, Yours Truly, and was based on a sample of Brenda Russell's 1979 hit "A Little Bit of Love," which became well-known to youngsters in the 1990s because of its use in rapper Big Pun's 1998 song "Still Not a Player." In the video, we see the couple cuddling while Ariana gushes, "I love the way you make me feel, I love it, I love it," and Malcolm encircling her waist. They ended the conversation with a passionate French kiss.

"The Way" did well commercially and peaked at number nine on the charts. Since he saw her as a true friend, Malcolm appeared happy. It was a mainstay on pop radio throughout 2013. He also thought she had real skill and was happy that her efforts to gain recognition as a musician were paying off.

Malcolm was still attempting to convince the critics, just like Ariana. He was still working on his new record, which he planned to release in June, in order to achieve this. He was referring to it as WMWTSO, or Watching Movies with the Sound Off.

Work on the album was driving him crazy. LA was a huge city with lots of people and places to go. He could get in his automobile at any time and go on an adventure. But instead, he went with the studio, a constrained, confined area, and the medicines, which made him introspective. He stayed up late. The hours went on forever.

Bruce Springsteen spent six weeks repeatedly recording the same snare drum for his seminal album Darkness on the Edge of Town. Jimmy Iovine, his engineer, believed he was completely insane. Bruce, though, resisted. He had a sound in his brain that he desperately wanted to capture on the record, but he was unable to do it no matter what he tried. till he did.

A rotating cast of celebrities, including Beyoncé, Jay-Z, Kid Cudi, Drake, DJ Premier, the RZA, and dozens of others, participated in the recording sessions for Kanye West's 2010 album My Beautiful Dark Twisted Fantasy, which cost him upwards of three million dollars. And Dr. Dre continued to work on Detox!

Malcolm read YouTube comments, and Kalson recalled how the unfavorable ones hurt him. Poor reviews undoubtedly affected him. He might have assumed Rostrum was at least partially at fault, which is probably unfair.

Like Macadelic, Watching Movies with the Sound Off was darker and rougher than the music Malcolm had grown to be renowned for; it was Malcolm with something to get off his chest; full of hubris, a blend of fury and aggravation. The record may have been his last-ditch effort to gain respect in a field that was all too quick to shun dishonest performers.

But Malcolm coveted the Fader cover, like it was something he wanted to cross off his bucket list. Even if they didn't like him, he wouldn't let it stop him.

Artie Pitt offered a cover story to Fader while Watching Movies with the Sound Off was being prepared for publishing, despite knowing that Malcolm was unpopular with the magazine. The crew had never been warm to Malcolm, but they had to admit that they now found his most recent compositions to be noticeably more fascinating. They therefore gave him some thought for the August–September 2013 issue. Even yet, they weren't entirely convinced and initially declined. Malcolm then went into full-on overdrive.

Malcolm then presented his case. He expressed his gratitude to Cohn for Fader not merely adoring him out of obligation and for not being "yes men" like many other media outlets in the cozy, back-slapping music industry. He didn't want to be simply another white rapper cashing in on hip-hop; he wanted Fader to know he was a true musician who dedicated everything to the creative process. "What he really wanted to impress upon me was that he was not the same artist he was two years ago and that he understood why it didn't necessarily connect right away," Cohn remarked. He had a strong sense of self.

The music reviewers he charmed would invariably produce positive articles, but Noz was resistant to being persuaded. He was a professional skeptic who had little faith in Mac's overtures and claimed in a column for the Fader that the critics had not misunderstood his work at all; rather, he said that it was awful and only in the worst possible ways derivative of the nineties. He believed that if Malcolm had been called a frat rapper, it was probably because he actually was one, at least at the time.

But there was something redeeming about his new music. According to Noz, Watching Movies with the Sound Off didn't have any hits. That was its charm, too. He referred to it as "deeply insular," noting that it was the kind of music that, in the 1990s, would only have been shared among friends via dubbed cassettes, as if to say: Check this out.

This, Noz appeared to imply, was more true to Malcolm's character or, at the very least, more appropriate for the man he was becoming into. This individual, who was no longer a young person writing boom bap songs and was now a resident of Los Angeles, surrounded himself with some of the most innovative hip-hop artists of the day, and appeared to cherish the chance to win over his detractors. The struggle itself was worthwhile.

All, though, weren't sold. Your hapless narrator gave the album a review for Vibe. I thought that while the album was good—the standout songs "The Star Room," "Objects in the Mirrors," "S.D.S.," and "Gees"—at times it was abstract to the point of being almost inaccessible. It also seemed to circle the drain on a subject that Malcolm was either unable or unwilling to fully address.

Even if the record suffered as a result, the heaviness was a sign of Malcolm's current state of mind, and he was powerless to change it. He claimed, "The more I make this sad music, the sadder I get."

There were references to more potent substances as well, such as fentanyl, a synthetic opioid that is fifty times more potent than heroin at the time and was only known to the most dedicated drug users. He raps, "Love me, love me, that fentanyl, it numbs me / Beautiful, it gets ugly, turns you into a junkie..." on the song "Someone Like You."

Chapter 15

In promotion of Watching Movies with the Sound Off, Malcolm went on tour. The thirty-eight-show run was named the Space Migration tour by the performer. He brought Earl Sweatshirt, the Internet, and Chance the Rapper as opening performers. In addition, he was trying to break a number of REMember Music acts, including the Come-Up, Njomza, Dylan Reynolds, Hardo, Choo Jackson, and Primavera Vills.

Malcolm had trouble filling arenas the last time he went on tour. Things got a little ugly when his recreational use of lean turned into a full-blown addiction. However, things were going well on this tour since he appeared to have a better handle on how to deal with his vices.

Space Migration was toned back with fewer concerts and smaller venues to account for what had happened when he tried to sell out arenas. His audience at the Hollywood Palladium was 3,800. Three thousand at The Hard Rock Live in Orlando, Florida. 1,400 at The Ritz in Raleigh, North Carolina. These were not large areas. However, smaller venues meant that spectators were packed in closer, and while performing he was closer to the audience. Like his first tours, this one had a fun atmosphere and felt more like a party than a concert.

He intended to make the tour enjoyable for the musicians who were performing with him as well as for the fans. He might have thought he was doing them a favor by giving them a chance to reach fans who might not have otherwise looked for them. Early in his career, he had a less than ideal experience because he was a supporting act himself.

The Internet and having a band were helpful. They revitalized Malcolm's sound, making it lush and organic, with Syd the Kyd (vocals), Matt Martians (keyboards/vocals), and Steve Lacy (guitar) as the band's frontmen. He enjoyed the idea that they were young people his age as opposed to musicians who spent their entire careers traveling and accepting every opportunity that came their way.

He traveled with MTV to Europe to film portions of the reality show's second and last seasons. In one episode, he travels to Ireland to research his Irish ancestry in between promotional appearances. He returns home in a subsequent episode, this time to pick up the key to Pittsburgh. When he returns home, he discovers that his grandmother has been compiling a scrapbook of everything he has ever done. He then makes stops at Timebomb and his former hangout ID Labs before receiving the key from Mayor Luke Ravenstahl, which his brother Miller, who was at that point employed as a graphic designer, was tasked with creating. When the mayor names September 13, 2013, "Mac Miller Day," viewers observe as Mac struggles to come up with a speech to receive the honor.

The cameras were criticized by other members of the Most Dope family, and Malcolm looked to be in agreement with everyone else at the moment. They would only be going about their daily lives, according to Bill. "And the MTV crew would halt them and request that they repeat an action. Oh, please repeat that and do it once more. They had grown weary of that.

Also, his well-being was a concern. When it came time to film the first season, he had obviously become somewhat more sober. Producers at MTV, however, privately voiced concern about Malcolm's welfare. He needed to be in the correct frame of mind before they started filming the show, but they still wanted to do it.

For many years, the connection was badly kept a secret. Nomi occasionally accompanied Malcolm on trips and went on tours with him. She had been obliquely mentioned in many songs. He also stated plainly that Macadelic was influenced by their highs and lows.

Though they had a troubled relationship, according to his acquaintances, he loved her more than anything. "He would have done anything for her," Clockwork added. Considering that this is Mac Miller, he didn't have to. He had the option of having any girl he desired at this moment. But he had a strong crush on her. He gave her his everything. When it came to her, he was benevolent. When he was traveling, he would send her flowers and shit. Every time she attended a show, he would change. She would simply bring the light; it had a positive energy.

She blatantly confessed her love for him in a post from October 2012, saying she didn't give a damn about their relationship's problems, including the fact that he was gaining fame while surrounded by other women.

According to her writings, the relationship had cooled off by the winter but had warmed up again by the time she left to Los Angeles for an internship in the spring of 2013. She adored her job, had her own apartment, and was nearer to Malcolm in LA. She was still uneasy.

She took care not to rely too heavily on Malcolm's assistance, though. Fine with the odd indulgence. But she looked resolved to accomplish anything more, like advancing her profession, on her own. Her independence was something Arthur Pitt remembered. She gave her writing her full attention, and most people around Malcolm thought she had a true gift for it.

But he was constantly putting up a show due to the obligations of his work. It might have been for her. possibly for different folks. Possibly even for himself at times. He was now playing a role, and it was difficult to distinguish between who he was pretending to be and who he actually was.

Even though he and Nomi were back together when he departed on a European tour in the fall of 2013, his relationship was still a major cause of worry. However, Malcolm still had other problems that bothered him.

The subject of how touring affected him is an intriguing one because it was one of the main ways that he and his business both made money.

Artie began sobbing in his Bedford-Stuyvesant apartment, but Malcolm ended 2013 having orchestrated one of the most amazing musical turnarounds. Along with the critically acclaimed release of Watching Movies with the Sound Off, he also produced the mixtape Stolen Youth, which many believe helped launch the career of Vince Staples. He also released Run-On Sentences Vol. 1, a beat tape, and Live from Space, a live album with five new songs, including "Life," the song he left off Watching Movies that finds him killing his girl.

Malcolm was close friends with ScHoolboy Q, Ab-Soul, Jay Rock, and Kendrick Lamar, all of whom were members of the TDE supergroup Black Hippy. They would also hang out at Malcolm's house. As a result of their regular chill sessions, many collaborations were formed, including one in which Ab-Soul recorded the majority of his third album, These Days, in the Sanctuary.

Friends like this undoubtedly had advantages. Apart from the movie, producing for other people pushed him to concentrate more intently on creating beats; the more beats he produced, the better he became. Delusional Thomas, one of his most intriguing ventures, is a mixtape. He had contributed to Watching Movies with the Sound Off by producing a few of the beats, but he was now fully in charge.

The lyrics on Delusional Thomas are painful and complicated, with each phrase carefully written to generate maximum shock and provide a glimpse into his shattered brain. It's an unpleasant and occasionally jarring listen.

Around the time Watching Movies with the Sound Off was being developed, work on Faces started, and it continued throughout the new year. Ballooners, a different project that was finished in late March, performed the same thing. For unknown reasons, he ultimately abandoned Balloonery in favor of Faces, which was released on May 11, 2014—Mother's Day—and the record has since been leaked online. Friends called it his "coke album" because Malcolm had returned to heavy drug use.

Even when he was lucid, he wasn't the friendliest person to be around because the drugs were taking control of him.

Furthermore, not everyone seemed to be concerned. Malcolm may have appeared to be heavily into drugs to those who are not familiar with him. He might have even felt that he was taking on too much. However, some of his close pals were much more addicted to drugs than he was, so he was considered a bit of a lightweight by them.

The song "Diablo," which features an epic exhibition of rhyming prowess over a piano loop lifted from Duke Ellington's "In a Sentimental Mood," is one of the mixtape's major highlights. He dedicated the video to his dog Ralphie, who had vanished during the recording of Faces. It was shot in front of an Echo Park pizzeria and featured his mom serving hot dogs and pickles from a food truck dubbed "Old Jewish" (which was also the theme of a limited run of T-shirts he made with brand Diamond Supply). Malcolm thought he had been kidnapped.[32] He was grieved by the loss of the dog, who, as he later discovered, had been devoured by a coyote[33]. This may have unintentionally added to the mixtape's gloominess.

Hunter S. Thompson, whose zany brand of first-person journalism seemed to seep into Malcolm's approach to songwriting; Charles Bukowski, the underground poet with his drunken bravado, whose character seemed to have merged with Malcolm's; and Timothy Leary, the shaman who prophesied the pleasures of psychedelics, were some of the record's more obvious influences. The mixtape allowed listeners to hear all of these voices practically; audio samples were inserted between songs to make the project's approximately 90 minutes flow together as one complete composition.

Last but not least, it's a pair of songs—sort of companions—that really go into what seemed to be happening when Faces was made. One of these is "Funeral," a throbbing march that serves as a sort of soundtrack to his own farewell—"play this at my funeral," he advises. Another is "Grand Finale," who is also preoccupied with dying and wants to be buried in Allegheny County, Pittsburgh, where he grew up.

He was worried he wouldn't make it in the real world. But everything was OK in the studio and the Sanctuary. He enjoyed it even though it was described as a dark, depressing area. It's ugly, but it's also bad, he remarked. "I'm not in a beautiful place, but I can look back and say—I did it, I made it out alive."

Chapter 16

Malcolm was residing in Brooklyn a year later. A two-bedroom, two-bathroom tri-level penthouse at 50 Bridge Street in Dumbo with a balcony overlooking the Manhattan Bridge and distant vistas of Manhattan had been substituted for the expansive Studio City residence. He had traveled to New York in a U-Haul with Nomi in tow from Pittsburgh, where he had spent the majority of the summer of 2015. He appeared committed to maintaining his union.

Will Kalson was recuperating and back in Pittsburgh. After starting a clothing line together, TreeJ and Peanut quarreled over its profits before TreeJ left for Miami and TreeJ returned to the 'Burgh. Big Dave was no longer in position. Jimmy Murton was on a quest for self-knowledge. Before his addiction problems sent him to prison, Bill Niels launched a clothing brand called Daily Bread with other pals.

After Blue Slide Park, Malcolm appeared to be destined for pop glory; he would be that white person who had a tenuous connection to Black rap but lived in a world that was predominantly white. Other white rappers were more than ready to enter the lane he had helped create for them after he refused it, though.

Although Macklemore was much older than Malcolm, they both came from Seattle, Washington, enjoyed underground hip-hop, respected the culture, and had independent success. The Heist was a huge success. There was no shortage of songs like "Can't Hold Us," "Thrift Shop," and "Same Love"—which he sang live at the Grammys while 33 same-sex marriages took place in front of the crowd.

A momentous year served as the backdrop for everything that was occurring. In the same year that Tamir Rice, Jerame Reid, Rumain Brisbon, Akai Gurley, Tanisha Anderson, Dante Parker, Ezell Ford, John Crawford III, and Tamir Rice were killed by police in Staten Island, Cleveland, and Cleveland, respectively, Akai Gurley was killed by police in Brooklyn, Tanisha Anderson was killed by police in Cleveland, Tamir Rice was killed by police in Cleveland, Jerame Reid was killed by police in Bridgeton, New Jersey, And those were the only murders that received widespread media attention.

However, it was the police shooting death of Michael Brown ("Hands up, don't shoot") and the Ferguson Uprising that fully crystallized the problems that had plagued Black America for more than 400 years in the most agonizing ways. The last thing anyone wanted to speak about was a white rapper sitting in his mansion, all alone, when it came to the value of a Black life. Malcolm was well and alive, but he wasn't... significant. The lack of white rappers.

"I fucking hate you, Donald Trump," Malcolm pleaded with the public on The Nightly Show with Larry Wilmore7. Additionally, he expressed open support for the Black Lives Matter movement, even asking on Twitter once what "white people who listen to rap" had done to help the cause. The sentiment was felt—what was happening in the world wasn't lost on him, and he wasn't so self-absorbed that he was oblivious to inequity and injustice. However, it wasn't evident what an accounting of his own efforts looked like. Even his self-awareness was growing, or at least his honesty about how his white privilege had helped him personally.

Even others had been moved by him. "Watching this kid—we have different upbringings, but it doesn't matter, he has a love and passion for music, for hip-hop, he doesn't belong, all this shit, and I'm looking at him like Yo, this is me," the rapper Logic stated. "When 'Donald Trump' was out, it was already over. I created ten "Donald Trumps" in an effort to emulate him. When Blue Slide Park first opened, I was on tour and we had a gig in Pittsburgh. I went to the park, went to the Frick Park Market, bought his sandwich, and then went to the park to eat it. I thoroughly enjoyed the album I listened to. I loved it even though many people didn't or claimed he went more pop.

He had achieved such popularity that Warner Bros. made him an unheard-of offer: 10 million dollars. That was quite an accomplishment for a young person from Pittsburgh who had done it all by himself. Did he want it, though?

Warner also handed him a deal for his record company, REMember Music, as is common in deals of this magnitude. He established the business as a side project in 2013 and paid for it himself. The label was determined to collaborate with the artists he had known personally and professionally from the Easy Mac days, like Vinny Radio, Franchise, Choo Jackson, Hardo, Dylan Reynolds, and Primavera Vills.14 He planned to give REMember's list of musicians some serious oomph with Warner on board.

The ethereal presence of Rick captivated Malcolm. This Long Island suburbia native couldn't play an instrument or use a mixing board, yet he nonetheless made it big in hip-hop by collaborating with Russell Simmons to found Def Jam. He later transitioned into rock production, working with everyone from Johnny Cash to the Red Hot Chili Peppers, and he had a natural talent for getting along with musicians and bringing out the best in them (including Kanye West's recently released Yeezus LP).

Their friendship grew swiftly, and Malcolm turned to him for support whenever he thought his drug usage problems were getting out of hand. While on tour in Europe, he was once "super wasted." He then dialed Rick.

Malcolm accepted Rick's invitation to stay at his house and in the summer of 2014 moved to a Malibu ranch with a private beach just a few blocks away from the producer's house. He would go to Rick's place every day that summer for some self-care, primarily transcendental meditation and cold baths.

The title of the debut single was "100 Grandkids." Sha Money XL, a music businessman who launched 50 Cent and G-Unit before gaining an A&R position at Def Jam, co-produced it. She was a huge fan of Mac Miller; in fact, he was so devoted that he attempted to persuade his superior, L.A. Reid, to work out a contract with Rostrum for Malcolm, but Reid was uninterested. Sha also included him in a case study that he gave Def Jam.

Malcolm had started to rely on the Clancys for counsel. He appreciated their desire to complete their tasks, but he kept the hell clear of them when it came to the creative process. Chris Clancy said on the Rap Radar podcast, "I'm not an A&R man, and I'm not trying to be an A&R guy. "If I like something, I'll tell you, and usually I'm wrong."

Chris Clancy didn't even initially like Malcolm. He described the rapper as "the white college guy who would go and sell out the House of Blues everywhere." "There were like four or five different versions of that." But the more they got to know him better, the more they could make out the vision. They quickly developed intense feelings for him.

Right there in front of Sha, Malcolm started putting his own equipment on. Big Jerm would later add his own spin. "Working with Em and Dre, we did that all the time," Sha remarked. We all contribute because we want to create music that is timeless.

Malcolm wanted to make a video for it when it was finished. It's a two-part clip, directed by Nick Walker, in which Malcolm sits in front of a lowrider and discusses the present in the first half while looking down on children performing in a play below. The song and the video in particular generated an impact thanks to its carnival-like mood.

But "100 Grandkids" was lighter, more enjoyable, and a throwback to Malcolm of Malcolm's early success. It appeared to be a brand-new chapter on a major label. He was fired up, laser-focused, and prepared to go.

He was keen to discuss drugs and how they had affected him when it came time to advertise GO:OD AM. He was therefore transparent when Fader approached him about producing a brief documentary called Stopped Making Excuses. He made it clear on tape that he preferred not to overdose over being perceived as a stereotypical white rapper.

People were praising the album. And by being honest about his struggles with substance usage, he won the admiration of many people going through similar things. He had to have made a good decision. The gloomy times weren't completely in vain. They aided the arts. "Mac was great at touching people, which was one of his strengths. He elicited emotions in people, according to Andrew Barber of FakeShoreDrive. People had a genuine belief that they knew him.

That didn't mean he took for granted the fact that his music could bring people together. He was aware of the fine line he was treading by utilizing drugs and alcohol to spark his creativity.

Chapter 17

Malcolm was scheduled to fly off for a string of performances in Europe on July 4, 2016. The trip had been canceled, and his team was on their way to see him while they waited for aircraft at the airport.

He was consuming copious amounts of cocaine to deal with the split, so much cocaine that Clockwork started to question if his friend, in whom he had always had such faith in his ability to maintain sobriety, might actually not be able to.

One of her friends claimed that Nomi's anger at Malcolm's drug use seems to have been a significant factor in her decision to stop things permanently. And in response to a question on her website, Taylor Magazine, she admitted that she dated "someone with some serious mental health and addiction issues for the better part of six years." She said that Malcolm had a "mental disease," and that taking care of his condition had worn her thin.

Since "The Way," Ariana's fame has increased thrice. She was quickly climbing the charts with Dangerous Woman when Malcolm was recording his Coca-Cola album Faces. But she had a thing for Malcolm all along. She was anxious to provide her support when she noticed that he was going through a difficult period.

Things rapidly became heated and intense. By the middle of July, they had been sighted together at Disneyland, and by the time paparazzi images of them sharing a kiss at the Japanese restaurant Katsu-Ya in Los Angeles appeared on TMZ in August, they had become a couple.

The images greatly increased Malcolm's profile. He was a well-known rapper who had achieved success, but his face didn't jump out at you as you waited in line at the grocery store checkout. Within a few weeks, the relationship had become well-known, and neither of them was skilled at talking about it.

Malcolm was also evasive. He was promoting The Divine Feminine, a concept album about love, his most recent release. It didn't take a genius to surmise that Ariana served as inspiration for the album given that he was going to release a single about love and that he appeared to be in love. She didn't, though.

Tyrone "MusicManTy" Johnson, who provided Malcolm a batch of beats before the song was created, is credited with starting the record. None of them appealed to Malcolm; he preferred concepts with a stronger musical element. MusicManTy then looked through his hard disk. He discovered something he had created in the wake of Stevie Wonder over ten years before.

Ty, however, had no idea where the files were. Since the original version only had live music, he had to start from scratch while creating the rhythm. "Nothing is looped," he declared. From the very beginning to the very end, I played every instrument. I began by saying, "OK, this is the verse and this is the hook," on the Rhodes [electronic piano]. I had no knowledge of how to loop, chop, or do anything similar when I first created it.

It takes a week of waking hours to match notes and sounds. Reusing a rhythm that an artist has already recorded runs the risk of making them fall in love with the original and think the new version doesn't measure up. Ty therefore put forth a lot of effort to perfect it.

CeeLo was one of the musicians with whom Malcolm had always wished to work. He liked CeeLo's development as an artist, from his beginnings as a rapper with the Goodie Mob to his transition into a genre-defying solo career before joining up with Danger Mouse to form Gnarls Barkley. Here was a man who was always moving.

Their collaboration, "We," stands out on The Divine Feminine, an album that shows a more experienced, sophisticated Mac Miller. Here was not the lyrical dynamo who had spent six years and hundreds of songs attempting to establish himself as one of the top rappers in the industry; rather, here was a performer in complete control of his voice who said only the words that were essential.

The words sometimes came slowly. He experienced a spell of writer's block while working on "Skin." He had been trying to think of anything important to say for two weeks. Then, out of nowhere, he came up with a verse and a chorus, only to leave the recording studio and discover that the singer Prince had passed away from a fake Vicodin that contained a fatal quantity of fentanyl.

The obscene "God Is Fair, Sexy Nasty," which features Kendrick Lamar, was another song that gained popularity. You might have anticipated a lyrical contest coming from two badass rappers. It was the exact reverse, though.

When Kendrick arrived in town to play on Late Night with Jimmy Fallon, Malcolm said the music was a real adventure to put together and was brought to life one night in the studio. As Kendrick listened to his new track, he appeared impressed.

The love between Malcolm's grandparents was so beautiful and pure that when he first heard the story, he started crying. During the fifty years of their marriage, Malcolm's grandfather never went to bed without telling his wife that he loved her. Malcolm claimed in a Vogue interview that he had spent his entire life seeking that kind of love.

An album that was very close to Malcolm—one of his purest artistic endeavors, almost self-indulgent in its goals—was enhanced by a special contribution from his grandmother. Robert Glasper, a pianist that Malcolm frequently hung out with, helped him bring it to life.

For nine months, Malcolm stayed sober. He stayed sober the entire Divine Feminine Tour, which ran from October through December. A perfectly tidy tour. No substances. No alcoholic beverages. Not at all.

It was challenging to become sober. He took his new sober coach, Shane Powers, to Lollapalooza as soon as he was discharged from rehab. A former Survivor candidate, nightclub promoter, and addict, Powers once relapsed so severely that he nearly snorted his father's ashes. He was charged by the Clancys with guiding Malcolm's behavior.

He had rented a home at 11659 Valleycrest Road in Studio City when he was back in Los Angeles. Compared to the mansion he had when filming the MTV show, it was a very different home. The three-bedroom, three-bathroom house, which was more suburban than Scarface, was located at the end of a peaceful block, was flooded with natural light, and featured wooden beams stretched over its vaulted ceilings, brick brickwork, and cedar hardwood floors.

These three children were very young—I saw them cross the street—about fourteen or fifteen. They might try to offer me candy bars, I believe. A child then commands me to give him anything I have. I may not have even had my wallet with me, but I had my phone. I had my dogs on a walk! I just got told, "I don't have anything." Then he produced the weapon. I believe I told her, "You don't want to do that." He interpreted that as me being hard. Hey, you don't want to shoot someone in broad daylight, was all I was trying to say.

He may have fallen into a depression as a result of his old enemy Donald Trump winning the presidency. Perhaps something else was involved. However, the gloom persisted long into 2017.

Malcolm accompanied Ariana on some of the dates of her Dangerous Woman Tour, joining her as she sang "The Way," which took place from the winter of 2017 through the fall of the following year. But he stayed back in the spring when she left for the European leg of the tour. After performing in Dublin, she traveled to Manchester, where on May 22, with more than 14,000 people celebrating inside the Manchester Arena and pink balloons falling from its rafters, an explosion occurred in the back of the arena. Her gigs in Stockholm, Oslo, and Amsterdam went off without a hitch. People were rushing about. There was blood all over. There was utter chaos. A suicide bomber had detonated a device. Over eight hundred individuals were hurt overall, and 23 people lost their lives. The youngest victim, who was only eight years old, was the youngest casualty, with ten people not even reaching their twentieth birthdays.

The episode severely devastated Ariana. She hadn't turned to music to inflict suffering. She had turned to music to spread happiness. Finally, this. She was so upset by what happened in Manchester that she worried she might never act again.

However, there were still issues. Malcolm was less wedded to the couch while he wasn't on the road performing than he had previously been. More often, he was leaving the house. He claimed he was going to a recording studio. But occasionally he'd disappear for three or four days. Nobody would also be aware of his location.

Later, Jerm recognized that Malcolm might have been using him as a buffer—a way to put distance between himself and those who had gotten too close—whether intentionally or accidentally. Although he was in an embarrassing situation, Jerm ultimately thought it was for the better. not only for him. However, Malcolm.

Jerm then thought he wasn't accomplishing anything on his own. Malcolm continued to depart. Furthermore, he wasn't including Jerm in the songs he was creating. Jerm guessed that the reason was because Malcolm wasn't skilled in the musical path he intended to take. Jerm was a recording engineer who had assisted Malcolm on countless sessions, thus he was more than just a producer. Throughout Malcolm's career, the ID Labs studio and production crew had been a constant, and he had previously referred to Jerm as the most soulful person he knew. There has to be something he could accomplish. He might not be able to make the rhythms, but he could provide his perspective. Malcolm had to be attempting to get away from him for a reason if he kept abandoning him at home.

Chapter 18

Malcolm nearly killed himself and his passengers when his G-Wagon collided with a light pole on May 17, 2018, then he fled into the night. When the police arrived at his home, he was taken into custody. He had almost twice the legal limit of blood alcohol in him.

Few days after the accident, Ariana started receiving texts accusing her. She responded by calling the relationship "toxic" and saying that no woman should feel like they need to be a mother or a babysitter.

The situation was quite convoluted. Fans were blaming Ariana, yet she had made significant efforts to convince Malcolm to stay sober. On his podcast, Shane Powers remembered how helpful Ariana had been in the beginning; he recalled that she would call him and ask how she could help. She was credited with aiding Mac's recovery, and he referred to her as a "stabilizing force."

A drug user? No way. He played music. an artist. a vocalist. a creator. and a plethora of other stuff. His way of life included doing drugs. In Hollywood, this was. This provided amusement. Everyone was doing drugs in this country, whether it was cocaine, crack, heroin, pills, lean, or molly. If not that, then at least booze, which was legal everywhere, or marijuana, which was legal in many locations at the moment. Everyone was in need of something. Anything to ease a life that, despite appearing to be simple, may nonetheless be quite difficult.

Others, however, weren't as persuaded. Clockwork was aware of the collision. And he recalled Malcolm's attitude toward it; just before he depressed the gas pedal, Malcolm had told him he felt "invincible." These were warning signs that were generally disregarded.

The show must go on, as the proverb says. In addition, Malcolm needed to create a new record away from the collision and the commotion it caused. Records didn't just appear. He had to spend hours, days, weeks, and even months in the kitchen to prepare the dinner.

He was then in Hawaii. capturing more. He was also working on several songs for singer-songwriters. While visiting a buddy who was trying to quit drinking, the producer Jon Brion, known for his work with Kanye West, Fiona Apple, and many soundtracks (most notably Eternal Sunshine of the Spotless Mind), had accidentally run into Malcolm.

Malcolm had dedicated his entire life to achieving this level of creative freedom. However, a number of the tracks remained incomplete. They differed only a little. Similar yet distinct. Less rapping, less funky, less dark—more singing. These were songs that might have been on a companion album. Circular swimming is what I do. The idea was that. two, possibly three albums. But undoubtedly two parts that came together to become a whole, showing Malcolm McCormick's dualities.

Now the medicines have returned. He was going to Chile with individuals that locals there did not know. They always knew that Malcolm's weird visitors were his drug suppliers whenever they were around. The atmosphere seemed odd.

He released a few singles—"Small Worlds" (with John Mayer on guitar), "Buttons," and "Programs"—to start building his buzz. His supporters welcomed them with open arms; they were viewed as a welcome return and a portent of good things to come.

Malcolm was performing on August 1. He was in the NPR offices, seated in front of a microphone, wearing a gray shirt over his slender figure and a brown dad hat.

Justus West on guitar, Klynik on keyboard, Joe Cleveland on bass, Kendall Lewis on drums, Robin Fay Massie on violin, YaShauna Swan on second violin, Lelia Walker on viola, and Melanie Hsu on cello supported him for his Tiny Desk Concerts performance. He had begged Thundercat to cancel a tour stop in Eastern Europe so he could be there that day, and the two of them would occasionally engage in humorous banter. Thundercat was at his immediate right.

Swimming has been discontinued for some time. Who could have predicted what it would do in the market. Who cares? Since the Rostrum era, the music industry has evolved significantly; first-week sales numbers are no longer as crucial as they once were. Now, streams were everything. DJs had been displaced by algorithms, radio had been replaced by playlists, and music reviewers had been destroyed by Twitter, Instagram, and Reddit.

But Bill was still interested in the beat. The songs he was writing explored addiction and trauma, two weighty subjects that pervaded his life. They were honest and passionate. Late in August, he texted Malcolm once more:

But being at home has its advantages. Artists stopped by the new property, despite its seclusion, much like they did when he owned the mansion in Studio City in the past. The rapper/singer Post Malone dropped by one evening in June, which sparked a jam session with him, Malcolm, Thundercat, and producer Frank Dukes (whom Malcolm had previously collaborated with but had never met).

The planned album was never recorded, but it seemed that Malcolm was now only at ease when he was being creative, whether that was in the recording studio or performing live. Like during his NPR Tiny Desk Concerts performance, where he was just off a coast-to-coast flight and seemed unaffected by anything while rapping about those years, which seem like such a long time ago.

He had encountered and, happily, survived a great deal of the terrible things that the crazy world brought. The drive to create compulsively was what caused him to open that door in the first place and what had led him down the paths—both good and bad—that his life had taken. He claimed that creation was the driving force behind everything.

Then came a run of brief performances. At the Hotel Cafe in Los Angeles, they were only for the fans. August 3–5, three evenings with his new band as he gets ready for the trip.

Even someone he hadn't seen in a long time was there. That had been occurring recently, much like the day he had reconnected with Nomi Leasure in a Brooklyn pub around that time, downing pale beers as she sipped martinis. Since moving out of the Dumbo apartment, they hadn't seen one another in two years. The night went on until the pub was about to close because there was a lot to unpack. At that point, she mentioned her new relationship and he appeared to be trying to put his former one behind him.

However, Nomi was not there that evening at the Hotel Cafe. That evening, Benjy Grinberg was standing there when Malcolm left the stage. Regardless of any disagreements they might have had, neither had ever spoken ill of the other. They were just two Jewish teenagers from Pittsburgh who liked hip-hop and went on to make history as a group. They hugged each other. Everything was done out of love.

After all, it was 2009 when he was looking for names while sitting on the porch of his parents' home. Malcolm was in need of a name for the team and the movement. There were numerous names on the table. But Q, an old acquaintance of his, had one that Malcolm in particular appreciated.

Malcolm was smitten. He suggested, "Let's go get tattoos." He was that sure and that convincing that he wanted everyone to have something permanent on their bodies that represented a concept that, in theory, hadn't even actually existed yet.

The entire crew then headed to Sinners & Saints Tattoo Shop in Pittsburgh's East End to make it official that very day.

He had management, a sober coach, and a devoted family. They could only do so much, though. They also had lives. The Most Dope Family, a large portion of his close acquaintances, had vanished. They were excluded from Malcolm's circle for reasons that, to them, were never really evident since they were preoccupied with other pursuits, consumed with their own troubles, or both.

Malcolm McCormick unlocked the door for the final time on September 7, 2018, early in the morning, two days later.

He was at home at last.

Printed in Great Britain
by Amazon

61239636R00067